AppSource

Discover How 10 Successful iPhone App Entrepreneurs Hit It Big Outsourcing The Development of Their Apps

Shane Lee

Praise for *AppSource*

"Great insight from those that have really done it—including the real value of an NDA and the necessity of a marketing and monetization strategy. The days when you could just drop an app in the App Store and make money are over."

- **Amber Sawaya**, Author of the Best Selling book, *Building a Mobile App: A Resource Guide for Clients & Corporations.*

"Fantastic book! Tons of useful knowledge you won't get in a classroom! The interviews give you a real personal feel to how to succeed on the app store. I highly recommend!"

- **John Bura**, Top Selling Udemy Instructor & Founder of Mammoth Interactive

"Shane Lee has done it again! His second book AppSource gives first-hand accounts of how app developers have used outsourcing to build highly successful apps and app businesses. The true stories are inspiring, realistic and packed with valuable information. A must-read for any app developer that wants success in the highly competitive iOS AppStore."

- **Jeff Hughes**, Author of *iPhone and iPad Apps Marketing: Secrets to Selling Your iPhone and iPad Apps*

"This book is a must-read if you do or ever want to do any outsourcing. There are lessons in this book that could save a lot of headaches when outsourcing and managing virtual workers."

- **Rob McCrady**, Developer of *Infinity Control* and *WordFlu*

AppSource: Discover How 10 Successful iPhone App Entrepreneurs Hit It Big Outsourcing The Development Of Their Apps

Copyright © 2013 by Shane Lee

All Rights Reserved.

No part of this publication may be reproduced, stored in a retrieval system or transmitted, in any form or by any means without the prior written permission of the author, nor be otherwise circulated in any form of binding or cover other than that in which it is published and without a similar condition being imposed on the purchaser.

For more information, please visit

www.beginningiosdev.com

Table of Contents

Foreword..6

Introduction: Can You Outsource Mobile App Success?.9

Chapter 1: Andreas Kambanis — Taking Bike Doctor To The Top Of The Sports Category......................13

Chapter 2: Chad Mureta — Outsourcing His Way To A Multi-Million Dollar App Empire......................23

Chapter 3: Chris Maddern — A Serial Technology Entrepreneur Falls In Love With Outsourcing.................37

Chapter 4: Jon Stinson — How A Music Producer Outsources iOS Games On The Side 49

Chapter 5: Petr Fodor — Quitting A Lucrative Job In Advertising To Develop Power Of Logic......................63

Chapter 6: Austin L. Church — From Getting Laid Off To Building A Successful App Development Company...73

Chapter 7: Matt Geoffrey — Making $1.6 Million In App Profits After Nine Months...........................86

Chapter 8: Isabelle Thomas Duston — The MBA Who Started An App Development Company................... 99

Chapter 9: Michael Jacobs — Simplifying The Process Of Networking With SociaLink.. 108

Chapter 10: Mike Milo — Outsourcing A Cash-Positive App Business That Helps Change The Lives Of Children Around The World 118

9 Outsourcing Hacks For App Development 134

About the Author 156

Foreword

For every rock star basking in luxury and glory, how many musicians struggle to make ends meet? For every hit that makes its author millions of dollars, how many great songs languish unplayed? I bet the answers to these questions are very discouraging, we all know that making it in the music industry is extremely challenging.

The good news is that nowadays anyone can get to the top of the Billboard charts, thanks to innovations in technology that redefined how music hits are made: who can bring their songs to a large audience, how quickly a catchy tune can reach billions, and how success is monetized. Just think of a singer previously unknown outside of his native Korea who became an instant celebrity and made tons of money with just one song. Alas, technology did not change the odds of a song becoming a hit and while money and fame are anyone's game, to win in that game one has to compete with the entire world.

Writing a mobile app hit is as complex as writing a hit song. With the number of apps on iTunes alone pushing one million, coming up with an idea that hasn't already been implemented—maybe even a few times—is hard. One might think of the mobile app industry as yet another Gold Rush story with chances of making any money pretty much gone by now. But there is a profound difference: unlike California's gold supplies that were quickly exhausted, the opportunities in creating new apps are limited only by our imagination. And consumers will always want—and buy—new, fun, helpful, engaging apps that capture their attention and pique their interest.

And even if you have a terrific idea for the next killer app you need to remember that the most innovative idea is merely the first step in a process that demands solid and swift execution. You must bring your idea to the market quickly, with level of quality that meets challenging benchmarks established by the best app developers in the world.

You might be the most creative person in the world, but if you have a lousy grasp of technology, little experience in digital arts, and think that Objective C is a grade you earned in school, how can you bring your idea to market? The answer is simple: let the pros handle it—outsource your app development.

Outsourcing—hiring someone to do the work you're not good at or prefer not to do for any reason—is a powerful tool. Outsourcing can reduce costs and time to market, improve productivity and quality, and provide access to hard-to-find resources.

But don't be naïve here. Outsourcing isn't easy and diving in it headfirst could cost you an arm and a leg. We've all heard stories about outsourced projects gone wrong. Nevertheless, in your case outsourcing could be the best—or only—way to deliver a winning app in the extreme pressures of today's market.

Outsourcing app development doesn't necessarily mean offshore outsourcing—plenty of mobile development companies have local technical teams. However, if cost is a sensitive issue, you might find yourself working with developers located thousand miles away, in a different time zone, with less-than-perfect English skills. These factors add complexity to your project.

To succeed with outsourcing your app development, it helps to know about the processes and procedures common to the software industry, and how to adjust these processes, procedures, tools, and techniques for outsourcing. This knowledge is an important ingredient for your success, but it's hardly sufficient.

With outsourcing, experience and luck count. But don't be dismayed, because with outsourcing, like other endeavors, the harder you work, the luckier you'll be. If you're inexperienced, learning from others—like the entrepreneurs in this book—can help. In fact, by reading these case studies, you'll get not just one coach, but 10—people who won and continue to win the mobile app game. These are real people who started with little to no knowledge of app development and outsourcing, faced challenges, and achieved success.

However, *AppSource* doesn't just tell you encouraging stories. Sure, you'll hear rags-to-riches tales and riches-to-greater-riches reports. But *AppSource* gives you deeper insights into the thinking and decision-making processes that resulted in these success stories. Through a series of in-depth interviews, Shane Lee uncovers secrets that can help you make or break your mobile app strategy; tools and techniques that will drive your hiring and management; and tricks, traps, and tools of the trade. These entrepreneurs share their hard-earned experience about how to name your app, create a marketing campaign, organize the app launch, incentivize freelancers, and more.

Writing a hit song or creating a popular app isn't easy, and not everyone will be successful. But if you have a great idea, work hard, get expert help, and follow the advice of those who've been there, your chances are better than most. This book will help.

Good luck!

Nick Krym

Author of *Outsource It!: A No-Holds-Barred Look at the Good, the Bad, and the Ugly of Offshoring Tech Projects*

Introduction: Can You Outsource Mobile App Success?

"Do what you do best and outsource the rest."

- **TOM PETERS**, Management Guru

You've probably picked up this book because:

1. You've got a nifty idea for an iOS app but you don't know the first thing about coding or developing a mobile app.

2. You're an indie developer who has released a couple of apps, and you're thinking of the fastest way to scale up your business.

3. You're a moderately successful mobile app development company looking to outsource a few more functions of your business.

Whatever the case, you're interested in finding out how other successful developers go about hiring out some, if not all of the functions of app development. Even if you have the creative and technical competence to handle building your app from start to finish, it still makes sense for you to outsource aspects of the work you may not be as competent in, or that you'd prefer not to handle.

There's no shame in not being able to do everything yourself. There are very few people in this world who can be world-class in more than one area, and it'll most likely be beneficial for you to stick to the area where you have the most experience. In my previous book, *The App Store Playbook*, I spoke about the direction in which the industry is heading, and how the App Store as we know it will be a vastly different organism in the next three to four years.

With the number of apps in the App Store at more than 900,000 and rising, it's an understatement to say that competition in the mobile space is stiff. Many of the developers I've spoken to have expressed the sentiment that the day of the solo bedroom app coder has come and gone. Quirky novelty apps with shoddy mechanics and little functionality can no longer survive in today's App Store.

The developers who will survive and thrive will be those that find an elusive combination of a fantastic product, great execution, and marketing savvy. This bodes well for the behemoths of the mobile industry, who wield the budget and clout to get every aspect of their app development right.

Unfortunately, independent developers with smaller budgets are going to be marginalized. We bandy about terms such as 'word of mouth' and 'going viral', but the reality is that for the mobile apps being released today, it's a lot harder to get increasingly jaded users to talk to other people about your apps, no matter how amazing they may be.

To even stand a chance, indie developers have to switch their mindsets from making an app to the best of their abilities to making the best app that they possibly can. Now, more than ever, outsourcing is essential to making this happen.

Why I Wrote This Book

In many of the interviews I've conducted for my website, www.beginningiosdev.com, I've noticed a common trend amongst successful developers. While many of them are highly competent in one area, their pursuit of perfection in that one area usually leaves

Introduction: Can You Outsource Mobile App Success?

them lacking in other aspects necessary to launch a successful app. The best developers recognize this, and understand that in order to succeed, they sometimes have to relinquish control of part of their apps to those with the skills to make it shine.

I started out by learning the fundamentals of iOS programming. While I believe it's absolutely necessary to understand the very basics, I acknowledge that I'm not a natural programmer, and that I'd get the best results by having the coding outsourced. I had previous experience outsourcing graphic design and web development, but this was a different ballgame altogether. I started scouring the web, reading books, and generally devouring all the material I could find on the subject.

While there are some great resources regarding this, I wondered how many successful developers actually engaged outside services to build their apps.

- Would their margins be too thin?

- What roles did these developers actually play?

- What aspects did they usually hire out?

Similar to the process of how my first book came about, I had many burning questions that needed to be answered. Due to my personal circumstances, I was particularly interested in speaking to indies that outsourced most of the coding and design functions. Unfortunately, unlike my first book, it proved a little harder to seek out noteworthy developers that did this, as admitting that two prepubescent Indian boys from Delhi built the core of your business isn't something that you'd usually shout from the rooftops.

AppSource

The ten developers featured all come from different backgrounds. Chad Mureta came back from a disastrous car accident to run a few multi-million dollar app businesses. Isabelle Thomas put her world-class MBA to good use managing the business side of her app empire. Mike Milo identified a need for speech therapy apps through his wife's practice. The one thing that unites them is that they have found a way to manage a profitable app business with outsourced help.

There are many things that a developer can hire out–programming, user interface design, graphic design, audio production, copy, video trailers, app marketing, etc. You might choose to find help for a couple, or all of these elements, depending on the complexity of your app, and the size of your budget.

Despite its ubiquity, outsourcing doesn't just have to mean heading to oDesk or Elance and getting some random third-world country worker to do your bidding. Get referrals from friends, collaborate with others, and barter services–there's more than one way to skin a cat.

While this book isn't meant to be an in-depth guide on how to outsource your app, we will lay out a brief blueprint on why and how you can go about doing this.

There're no hard and fast rules on outsourcing the many different areas of app development (or building a mobile app development business for that matter) but the experiences of the afore-mentioned developers should provide some guidance on how to go about doing so.

Chapter 1
Andreas Kambanis

◆

Taking *Bike Doctor* To The Top Of The Sports Category

Andreas Kambanis is the founder of the popular cycling blog, London Cyclist. Originally a hobby blog, Andreas got serious with the website after getting frustrated with his day job in a market research company.

Combining his passions of blogging and cycling, he has added developing mobile apps and writing ebooks to his lifestyle business. Realizing that many iPhone users are also avid cyclists who need simple bike maintenance manuals, he outsourced the development of *Bike Doctor* and the rest, as they say, is history.

On the day *Bike Doctor* was launched, it hit the top of the sports category and shortly after, received a feature from Apple, turning over $10,000 in revenue in its very first month.

***

Q: Hi Andreas. Could you please tell us a little about your background and how you got into iPhone app development?

A: I run one of the world's most popular cycling blogs, London Cyclist, and I spotted a few pain points for cyclists. One of them

AppSource

was knowing how to complete repairs yourself so you can save money. This led me to develop a solution called Bike Doctor that teaches people how to repair their bikes. Most of my apps have come from a deep knowledge of the cycling market and the problems cyclists face.

Q: Spotting pain points for a niche market and developing solutions for them. That should be a startup mantra right there. From what I understand, you outsource the entire programming and design aspect of your apps. Have you had any difficulties in communicating exactly what you wanted to do while doing so?

A: Yes, communication can be a problem. This is why I now focus on using Eastern European developers who seem most able to understand and follow my instructions. Problems in communication generally come from situations in which something that I believe is very obvious and clearly instructed is mistranslated by someone else.

I recently needed a very simple new splash screen to appear on an old copy of *Bike Doctor*. I requested this work from a graphic designer and expected it back by the end of the day. Around two days later, I received a complete app re-design that was completely different from what I requested! Granted, it looked good, but he completely ignored my brief.

Q: That sounds like a pretty bad mix-up. What do you think are the best ways to deal with these communication issues?

A: You'll quickly discover if you've got communication issues with a developer. This is a red flag and it signals that it's time to seek out a developer who is better at communicating with the client. To

Chapter: 1

> get around these issues, I try to explain things in as much detail as possible, going beyond what I would explain to a natural English speaker.
>
> I always emphasize to the developer to ask any questions with anything they need clarification with. This encourages them to ask questions as opposed to just guessing. If you are worried about whether a developer will be able to handle a big project, you can assign them a small task first and see how they get along with that.

Q: How do you manage your developers and source code? Do you use any project management tools?

> **A:** Odesk and ELance have some fairly good communication tools built in to their service. This is where I do most of my communication with developers. Occasionally, especially at the start of the project, I'll hop on Skype to talk to the developer about what we're trying to achieve with the project.

Q: Do you only take over the code at the end of the project?

> **A:** I generally have nothing to do with the code. It is sent to me so I have a copy, but I'll get the developer to do all of the uploading to the App Store.

Q: How necessary do you think a Non Disclosure Agreement (NDA) is for someone outsourcing development of an app?

> **A:** I don't think it's necessary at all. These are largely not worth the paper they are printed on. If it makes you sleep better at night, use one. I'd personally rather protect my market position through

constant innovation of my apps and having a more advanced marketing process.

Q: Do you think that you're at any sort of disadvantage without understanding the basics of iOS programming? How do you mitigate the risk that the programmers you hire might possibly take advantage of this situation?

A: Yes, sometimes programmers can take advantage of this a little. I remember working with a developer and asking him to reduce the size of the app. He said it wasn't possible. I looked through the folder containing the app and saw that a number of files were saved as a BMP file format, taking up an enormous amount of space. I quickly asked him to replace them with JPGs. It's crazy that he didn't think of this solution himself. This is just a simple example but on a wider level developers may say "oh, that's not possible" when most of the time it is. They either just don't know how to do it or they can't be bothered to. When this happens, thank them and find a new developer.

Q: Yup, that's why they say you should be 'slow to hire, quick to fire'. Given that you've had a fair amount of experience outsourcing your projects, what would you say would be the best practices for hiring a coder?

A: Only hire people with very high feedback ratings and make sure you interview before you hire. Usually there'll be one developer who really stands out. Also, make sure you invite lots of people to bid on your project, as this will give you a wider number of developers to choose from.

Q: How has *Bike Doctor* done to date on the App Store in terms of sales/downloads?

Chapter: 1

A: We managed to get 8,000 downloads of the paid edition. We also recently went free and got around 4,000 downloads on that too. We'll be switching back to 'paid' shortly.

Q: Did you expect *Bike Doctor* to be as successful as it was? What do you think you did right with the app and why?

A: *Bike Doctor* solved a real problem people had. It was easy for Apple to feature it, as it was and is a great app. It's incredibly useful for someone who downloads it. I also nailed the marketing process. I built up a launch around the app and emailed everyone on my email list when it launched. That gave it that big initial volume to climb up to near the top of the paid sport category.

Q: If you were starting out in iPhone app development again, what would you do differently?

A: I wouldn't partner with someone to create the app. Instead, I'd simply hire a developer as looking back, it wouldn't have cost me more than $2,000 to develop.

Q: Do you think there's a formula for success on the App Store? If so, what do you think that formula is?

A: Yes. The secret is in the launch. That's where you have your greatest leverage. You should aim to have a big list of people you know who will download your app in the first 24 hours. You do this by building interest prior to launch or partnering with someone who has a huge audience you know you can tap into. This propels you into the limelight and puts your app in the top charts. From there, there's a domino effect. It increases the chances of getting your app noticed by Apple and being seen by more people.

Q: What were your biggest challenges and lessons learnt from releasing your first app? Would you create the same app today in a different way?

A: To answer this one, let me talk about another app of mine, *London Bike Rides*. For this one, I actually hired a developer from Ukraine. There're two things I would have done differently. The first is to release a free edition with an in-app upgrade to get more 'rides'. This way I can draw people in and then hopefully convert them to paid customers. The second is to hire a designer separately. He could have made the app look far more stylish. There's a strong possibility I'll do this in future.

Q: That makes a lot of sense. Getting contractors who specialize in their respective fields is usually the way to go. Do you have a process for going from app idea to full-blown development?

A: To start with I play around with an idea for an app in my mind. I'll use other apps and try to picture how some of their features would work in my app. I'm always looking at other apps for design ideas and also for functionality. If other developers can do it, then I want to know how I can implement it in my app.

Once I've got the idea in my mind, along with some example screenshots from other apps to help me explain to the developer, I'll draft out a document that lists all the features. I'll also create simple screenshots using text boxes in Microsoft Word. All of this helps me make it as easy as possible for the developer to understand the app. Then, I'll interview and hire a developer and a designer.

Q: Do you conduct beta-tests with potential users for your apps? If you do, how do you go about it?

A: I'll recruit my friends and I'll also give away a sneak preview to a select group of my audience.

Q: Now that there are more than 900,000 apps on the app store, do you think that the market is becoming a bit too saturated for the average independent developer to succeed?

A: It's certainly not getting easier but it's still possible to be successful and there're still an incredible number of opportunities in the market. While the number of apps may be growing dramatically, so is the number of iPhone and Android users.

Q: Why do you think most indie developers seem to have such a hard time making a living from selling their own apps?

A: Because they believe in the maxim 'If you build it, they will come'. Not only do you have to build a great app that people want to use, you also have to find an audience for it. Once you've found the audience, you also need to have a way to connect with them. There are so many ways to do this. One that I employ is to have a popular blog. However, this isn't the only tactic I use and if you don't have a popular blog already, then that shouldn't stop you.

Q: What words of advice would you have for someone just starting out in iPhone development?

AppSource

A: Have an audience ready and waiting to download your app on the first day of your launch. If you've managed to collect the email addresses of, say around 500 people who are interested in your app, then you know you are on to a winner.

Q: I understand that you're a pretty big fan of Launch Rock and Punch Tab. What other online resources do you recommend for app development?

A: There're two important ones I'll mention here. App Design Vault has a number of themes available that you can use for your app. This is great if you are trying to save money by not hiring a graphic designer. It's also great for inspiration. You should also bookmark http://urbanairship.com/ as they offer an incredible API that you can include in your app to provide notifications.

Q: Do you do any marketing for your apps, and if so how do you go about doing it?

A: One of the main tactics I use is to cross promote apps. I'll do this through in app notifications. I know I've got a big audience of cyclists who've downloaded my previous apps so it's easy for me to drop an in app notification to let them know if I've launched a new app.

I also try to contact blogs of people whose audience I know will be interested in my app. If I do this, I'll always aim to address the blogger by name and write them a customized message. Copy and pasting a generic marketing email just doesn't work.

Q: Can you elaborate on why you use cross promotion as one of your main marketing strategies?

A: Sure. This is an incredibly important tactic. It can be expensive and time consuming to acquire a loyal user. Once you've got them and they are happy with one of your apps, the chances are they'd like to grab another one from you.

Q: Your strategy for a launch plan is interesting but what are your thoughts on bigger developers paying high amounts per user for the indirect benefit of being seen on the charts. Do you think it's an ethical practice?

A: I haven't ever personally used this tactic and I find it a little unethical. I think it's something Apple will be clamping down more on in future so I'd probably try to avoid using this tactic. There are more effective, long-term methods to use than to cheat your way to the top. I'd rather sleep each night with a clear conscience than worry about whether Apple will catch me.

Q: The buzzword for a while now in the app developer scene is 'Freemium'. Do you think that pursuing this strategy will continue to be feasible over the long haul? What are your thoughts on how app monetization will change in the future?

A: Absolutely, drawing people in with free features or part of your app is a great way to get them interested. Many people want to test things out before parting with any money. However, this isn't appropriate for all apps. If you are going to do this, the crucial aspect is to have a well-designed upgrade page. This will convince people to get the full version.

Q: How important do you think constant updates are in retaining users and maintaining downloads?

AppSource

A: It's important to pleasantly surprise your audience and give them reasons to talk about your app. Hence updates are important. Of course you should only do so if there are useful new features to add. I ignored this for a long time and I'm impressed that my audience has stuck with me, even as I failed to improve my apps. Now I'm over delivering on updates and I know this will get them talking about the app and make them happy they chose to be a customer of mine.

Q: What are your thoughts on the recent revelation that Apple is clamping down on app store rankings manipulation from bots and human armies?

A: Well done Apple! Their tight control can sometimes be a blessing and other times a nightmare. Fortunately in this scenario, I'm glad they are helping respectable developers to do good work. They know that the future success of the iPhone relies on people wanting to develop apps for it.

Q: Great! That's a wrap. Thanks for taking the time out for this interview!

A: My pleasure.

Chapter 2

Chad Mureta

◆

Outsourcing His Way To A Multi-Million Dollar App Empire

It takes a special type of person to bounce back from severe depression and a crippling $100,000 debt to build a few multi-million dollar businesses. It takes a person like Chad Mureta, who conceptualized his first hit iPhone app, *Fingerprint Security Pro*, from the confines of a hospital bed.

Originally running his own real estate business, Chad was forced to watch his livelihood slowly disappear after he was involved in a car accident that almost left him with one arm. Without anyone at the helm, his real estate business failed and the hospital bills started mounting.

In Chad's own words, 'It was the lowest point of my life.'

Fortunately, there was a light at the end of the tunnel. While recovering from a surgery to save his arm, Chad came across an article talking about entrepreneurs making money with mobile apps. With nothing left to lose, Chad borrowed some money from his father-in-law and outsourced the entire development of *Fingerprint Security Pro*, which ended up making more than $700,000 in revenue. Since then, he has gone on to develop a few more successful mobile app

AppSource

and software businesses, all without knowing how to program a single line of code.

***

Q: Hi Chad. Your story is an inspirational one. For the benefit of readers who don't know you, can you please tell us a little about your background and how you got into iPhone app development?

A: I've always had the 'entrepreneurial' drive in me. I held various jobs trying to find success and happiness, and eventually fell into real estate, which I thought was my ticket to all of the above. I soon found out that success equaled 12 hour days and absolutely no life outside of work. I was in that cycle of "if I just keep at it a little longer," thinking things would change, but they, of course, never did.

It's funny how life works though. I had one night off, for the first time in a long time, and chose to go to a basketball game with a friend in Charlotte. It was such a fun night, being able to hang out and kick back. That elated feeling got me thinking on the drive back about how I couldn't keep living the way I was living. It was depressing how that one night at a basketball game was the happiest I'd been in a long time. And just like that, a deer jumped out on the interstate, causing my car to swerve, hit the divider, and flip about four times. I don't remember too much, but I'll always remember looking at my arm. It was so mutilated, I couldn't even recognize it at first.

I was in and out of the hospital for weeks. Doctors were telling me that they couldn't save my arm. My real estate business was failing without me there. The hospital bills kept racking up. I ended up about $100,000 in debt and that wasn't even the end of it. I was in a severe depression. Luckily, things took a turn and an intensive surgery was able to save my arm. While in recovery, a friend visited me in the hospital and gave me an article to read called 'App Millionaires' telling me to seriously consider it. I read the article, which talked about entrepreneurs making money with apps, and how some of those entrepreneurs didn't have any tech experience. There were so many reasons I could have brushed it off and forgot about it, but at the time, I really felt that I had no other option and was searching for anything to pull me out of my situation. I jumped in with both feet and never looked back.

Q: And after jumping in, the very first app you developed, *Fingerprint Security Pro,* became a best seller on the App Store, netting you over $700,000 in profits to date. What were your biggest challenges and lessons learnt from releasing this app?

A: The biggest challenges were definitely learning the tech-side of things. I knew nothing, so I was starting from square one. But I was determined and I really enjoyed it, so I kept going. Also, app marketing is a completely different type of marketing, so I had to learn completely new concepts. People ask me all the time about web pages and social media marketing for their apps, which could bring in trickles of downloads maybe, but app marketing is really about what you do in the App Store and within your app.

AppSource

Q: How important do you think it is to have a project manager for an app business? At what stage would you advise a small setup to hire a project manager?

A: Yes, it's important but as you sort of mentioned, it depends on what stage you're at in your business. I didn't start out with a project manager because I was making one app to begin with. Then, I moved on to about two to three apps at a time. Once you start scaling, a project manager could be crucial to keeping your business running smoothly. With one of my earlier businesses, my partner acted more as the project manager and I worked on marketing and research. He was amazing at managing and I was able to focus on what I'm great at. I still use project managers now because I'm not just working on apps anymore. The more you put on your plate, the more you need to update and fine-tune your system.

Q: How necessary do you think a Non Disclosure Agreement (NDA) is for someone outsourcing development of an app?

A: I get this question all the time—"Will an NDA protect me in [country/state/etc]?" It's important for people to understand that technically, no, nothing can truly protect you. I've been screwed over and taken advantage of. Honestly, it's all a part of hiring. However, having developers sign NDAs, non-competes, making clear agreements, and keeping records of any conversations you have with your team is protection you can use *if* it comes down to legal action.

The best protection though is simply to hire smart. It's not always easy to find and hire developers, so people sometimes rush this process because they just want to get started or because the price is so cheap. Huge mistake! You need to hire slow, and fire fast. Think long-term relationships. You want to create an established relationship with your developer. You don't want to be another side-project for them. And this goes for how you treat your development team as well. Be professional.

Q: **Despite what you mentioned in your book on managing outsourced programmers, do you think that you're at any sort of disadvantage without understanding the basics of iOS programming?**

A: There've definitely been times when I wish I could have just shoved someone aside and started coding like a madman to get the job done. But in the long run, I believe being able to focus on marketing, research, and the business side of apps has been crucial to my success. It's also been a huge part of living the '4 Hour Work Week' lifestyle, which was always my goal. As you become more experienced, you definitely should learn more about iOS programming. Could I pick it up and code? Probably not, but I at least understand terminology and expectations. I know what to look for in a developer, what things cost and how much time things take. These aspects are the most important things to know in this business.

Q: **I agree. I think understanding the terminology and possibly even the fundamentals of iOS programming could be useful in that regard as well. You understand what you're looking for, and it's less likely that there'll be miscommunication if you know how to detail exactly what you require. You've founded and co-founded a number of mobile app development businesses. Is there a particular reason that you decided to set up multiple companies to develop apps?**

AppSource

A: I have a fear of commitment...

I'm just joking but in a way it's because I *did* want to keep moving on. I would build up one business and then be ready to let it go, *especially* for the amount of money other people were offering me. What I love about the app business is the freedom it gives you. You're not tied down to it, you don't have to sit at your desk and continue to build and build. But even with an app business, you have to keep monitoring and tweaking and monitoring and scaling.

You can't just throw your app into the store and put your hands up, expecting downloads and millions of dollars to flow into your pockets. You have to adjust your tactics with the market to keep downloads and customers coming back. Each time, I was ready to let go of these particular apps and pass on the tweaking and monitoring to someone else, so that I could build up new ones. I still enjoy the building and selling of app businesses.

Q: While I understand you've been very successful, what would you do differently if you had the chance to start out in app development all over again?

A: I would retain a development team sooner. Of course, you need to get your feet wet, but once I got the hang of things, I would have started to build a team right away. Preferably in-house. Your company becomes so much more of an asset in this respect. It takes more work, and a lot more commitment, but I believe doing this earlier on could have generated even more revenue in the long run.

Q: Do you think there's a formula for success in the App Store? If so, what do you think that formula is?

A: There're a couple formulas but these are evolving rapidly. I'd say one of the formulas is to emulate. A lot of people have trouble with this word. They get really angry and yell about innovation. What a lot of people fail to realize is that successful, seemingly innovative ideas are already based off others, and not even just with apps. If you take a look at the top paid, free, and grossing apps, you'll often find that you can play "name the related app" with each one.

Everyone is taking a popular idea and making it better. That's the best way to have a successful app and it's how I've always developed. You have to research the market and give them what they want. Why make an app that no one will download? There're obviously exceptions to the rule, but niche apps won't make you millions.

Another formula that's become more prevalent in the past year is high-quality graphics. If your app has an outdated icon or poor screenshots, it's not going to be downloaded. Your app can be simple in function, but it still has to have killer graphics.

Q: Those guys that get angry and yell about innovation take things a little too seriously, don't they? Personally, I don't have a problem with emulating successful apps but I do think there should be a distinction between emulating and ripping off. There're just way too many shoddy knock offs out there that are close to carbon copies of the original app with one or two minor 'tweaks'.

How do you go about conducting beta-tests with potential users for your apps?

A: The family and friends plan! At least with my first couple apps, I would give out the app to all my friends and family, but not tell them it's my app. I would watch as they played with it and asked them about their thoughts. It was really effective to watch and analyze for intuitiveness (super important) and overall functionality and appeal. I was able to test all ranges of ages as well. Another method I used for beta-testing was by putting it first into a single store, like Canada, and collect that data for optimization. Then update accordingly and put it on all the stores.

Q: Releasing an app in a single store and then collecting data on how users react to your app for optimization sounds like borderline genius! How much impact do you think this has on sales in other countries after you adjust your app based on the feedback you receive? Are there any negative effects if you don't have a full scale launch from the get-go?

A: I remember the first time I told people that, they thought it was the funniest thing to use Canada as a test market. But it works! My apps were optimized by the time they hit the largest markets, thus higher conversion rates. When I had the most eyeballs, my app was able to retain those customers. This means more downloads, more reviews, and faster ascension in the ranks. The negative would be wasting time for an app that would convert well from the beginning, but most apps don't start out perfect. Tweaking is essential.

Chapter: 2

Q: Now that there are more than 900,000 apps on the app store, do you think that the market is becoming too saturated for the average independent developer to succeed?

A: It's definitely more difficult, but mobile is going in so many directions that there's still an incredible amount of potential. Keep following the market and watch for trends. Don't hesitate. Make your moves and get your apps out there. The longer you wait, the harder it will be.

Q: So how do you think independent iPhone developers can succeed going forward?

A: I'd say that as an independent developer, you should never underestimate the power of numbers. You need to grow your network and work with other developers, as that will be your most powerful tool.

Q: Why do you think most indie developers seem to have such a hard time making a living from selling their own apps?

A: I feel that a lot of developers don't research the market enough. I get hundreds of emails a month asking me to help them with [insert revolutionary app idea], but there're two things people fail to consider:

   1) Your app idea might not be as great as you think it is.

   2) It's not about the idea. It's about execution.

AppSource

So many developers will put a great app on the market and not understand why it's not successful. It's because the path to app success is so much more than just the 'idea'. I like to give people this reference that a friend brought up to me–if someone told you three years ago that they would make millions on an app where you shoot birds at pigs, would you have believed them? Probably not. Rovio nailed the execution, it didn't matter if it was shooting angry duck feet at purple dinosaurs. They knew how to execute and market their app successfully.

Q: So true. What words of advice would you have for someone just starting out in iPhone development?

A: Do your research, don't fall in love with your idea, and move quickly. A lot of people wait for their app to be perfect before releasing it. They're losing valuable analytics by doing this. They can update their app as they go along, while collecting crucial data that they can analyze and then implement. A published app is better than an app in progress any day.

Q: What do you think are the advantages/disadvantages of focusing on the iPad?

A: The iPad is growing really fast so it's a hot market, and it opens up doors for different types of apps that mobile phones just won't do justice. The disadvantage is the reach. The iPad will never be as heavily used as the iPhone. I'm not carrying my iPad in my pocket. The iPhone is like an umbilical cord for most people. Plus, the most up-and-coming users (Africa, India, and Asia) aren't buying iPads, they're buying smartphones.

Chapter: 2

Q: What's currently your favorite iOS app, and why?

A: This is going to sound lame because people expect something they haven't heard of, but I'm a practical guy. My favorite apps are mobile car apps, such as *Uber* and *Lyft*. I'm all over the place so these apps are extremely useful. Both have developed a distinct customer experience and are very easy to use.

Q: What is your development setup like? How large is your development team?

A: Like I mentioned earlier, I don't just work solely on apps anymore. So my development team works on other projects as well, and my overall team is larger than when I was a sole developer. I have a network of about five to ten people (depending on the project) that I use for software and apps. I never use them all at one time, but that's actually the model I'm moving towards.

Q: I've learnt a lot from reading your book. It's a great read. In the book, you mention using paid traffic to grow your business. Unfortunately, most of the indie developers I've spoken to have reported largely negative experiences when purchasing traffic. Would you like to elaborate on what you consider to be the best practices in this area?

A: Definitely. In my book I state, 'only use this strategy after exhausting all free tactics' and what I mean by 'exhaust' is only after *properly* implementing all free tactics. Optimize your app before ever spending money on traffic. If you put your app on the store and then pay for traffic right away to get downloads, you won't be retaining anyone and it will drop very suddenly. This is

AppSource

because paid traffic won't help a newbie or poorly marketed app, it will only help what's ready for all those eyes and downloads.

Q: What are your thoughts on bigger developers paying high amounts per user for the indirect benefit of being seen on the charts? Do you think it's an ethical practice?

A: Well, it's business after all. We live in a capitalist environment, I wouldn't have expected anything less. Of course, I don't want it to get out of hand. There should always be some regulation for the little guys because that leaves so much more room for possibilities, but we'll see.

Q: The buzzword for a while now in the app developer scene is 'Freemium'. Do you think that pursuing this strategy will continue to be feasible over the long haul? What are your thoughts on how app monetization will change in the future?

A: Yes, I definitely believe in the Freemium model. Most people want to put their app out there for $0.99 or more because they don't understand that the app market is still in its infancy and that's too 'expensive' for the average user. You're putting up walls to your app that don't need to be there. Offer your app as a freemium and you will get way more customers. Someone will not purchase your app, but if it's free, they have no reservation, and if your app is good, they'll realize that they actually do want to upgrade, buy more, etc. Freemium apps make more money and get more downloads.

As for the future of monetization, I think it will begin to turn into a more subscription based model–monthly, yearly fees, etc. I also think geo-location will play a big part. You'll see prompts when you're close to somewhere or in certain stores.

Q: I was actually just speaking to another developer about how subscription based models don't seem to be translating to the App Store so much even though it's so prevalent on the web. Do you have any thoughts on why not many developers are looking at this model, and how it can become more feasible?

A: I think the reason for this is because it's a future model. The App Store is still so, so new. Apps are everywhere so people often forget that this is just the beginning. The current model will be around for a bit longer before it converts to anything else. Right now, it's just too young. I know a few people who already use and love some subscription apps though. It's just not the norm, so I wouldn't move that direction until the market was pointing that way.

Q: In your book, you also mention growing your developer network and getting other developers to cross-promote with you. For new developers starting out, how would you advise them to do this in the most efficient manner?

A: You have to put yourself out there. I was at every conference and signing up for tons of Meetups wherever I was. I grew a network and established invaluable relationships. I had an unbeatable mastermind group and together we were killing it with apps. Recently, I've started a developer network for App Empire appreneurs who have taken my app course. There're about 1500 members all working together and sharing their experiences and lessons. It'll be critical to their success, especially for those who are new to the business.

AppSource

Q: What are your thoughts on the recent revelation that Apple is clamping down on App Store rankings manipulation from bots and human armies?

A: I knew they would be doing this, so I'm not surprised, it was just a matter of when. With any platform, people will find their ways around it, but I don't worry too much about it since that's not the way I work. I don't teach others to use those tactics either as it's more trouble avoiding the hammer from Apple than just following the guidelines. The same goes with copyright laws (another question I get all the time). Read Apple's Developer Guidelines! I can't say it enough. So many developers build an app and then realize, "oops, that's not allowed." If you start by complying with their guidelines from the beginning, you can avoid time and money lost.

Q: OK, thanks so much for your time Chad. I'd wish you the best of luck but it sure doesn't look like you need any!

A: No problem. Thanks for having me.

Chapter 3
Chris Maddern

◆

A Serial Technology Entrepreneur Falls In Love With Outsourcing

Usually, most people with development backgrounds tend to focus their energies on the programming aspects as opposed to outsourcing. Not Chris Maddern.

Having founded his first startup in college, Chris Maddern fell in love with entrepreneurship and never looked back. He is the Chief Technology Officer of *Corkbin*, a wine memory and sharing platform for the iPhone, and the co-founder of App Launch. A serial technology entrepreneur, Chris is currently obsessed with mobile technology.

His first successful venture into app development started with *iCarCheck* and he is currently involved with a number of other projects, including AppsForGlass, the first portal for Google Glass Apps.

***

Q: Hi Chris. Let's start off by finding out more about your background and how you got into iPhone app development?

AppSource

A: I actually have a pretty unusual background for outsourcing. I come from a development background and am a serial technology entrepreneur. I joined *Corkbin* a little after it was first conceived, when development was already underway with our outsourced team. However, I have worked closely with them on new products, and closely evaluated the process.

I first started app development a few years ago when a few friends and I decided we wanted to tackle a problem we saw in the UK vehicle data market (think CARFAX). It's expensive and it's essentially got one colluded artificial price point. We wanted to change that and saw mobile, as an emerging technology, to be a chink in their armor so it was a big part of our strategy. I made *iCarCheck* mostly by myself over the next few months and fortunately, when we launched it was a success. We were able to grow *iCarCheck* into a reasonably-sized business.

Since then I've never looked back and spend all of my time developing mobile products—in this industry, if you execute well, you stand as good a chance of succeeding as anyone.

Q: That's a great story and having a development background is perfect for outsourcing if you ask me. I'm from the camp that you need to have done and understood the work to be able to delegate it the most effectively. That said, have you had any difficulties in communicating your requirements? From what I understand, you outsource all the programming and design aspects of *Corkbin*.

A: This used to be true. We're now bringing more and more functions in-house as resources allow. This doesn't have anything to do with any problems with the status quo. Rather, because we are a technology company with domain expertise, a large part of our value is in being able to execute on new wine-related tech very quickly, specifically around recommendations we're moving into. We need expertise in-house to grow the product more quickly without having the issue of cost trump speed.

Also, try raising venture capital funds by saying that the technology company that they're potentially going to invest in, is just going to pay someone else to make the product–I dare you!

We have actually had nothing but great experiences with Inmite–a development agency based in Prague–they have been supportive, facilitating and more importantly, have shipped every step of the way with consistently high quality. As we've started to take over the code base, there have been very few surprises–which is rare.

That said, outsourcing is like many things in life; you get out some function of how good your initial choice was, and how much effort you put in. The people you outsource work to don't necessarily share your vision–in some cases Inmite actually did, but you can't assume–so you have to be clear, provide specifications, give feedback early and often, and make sure that they really understand what it is that you're trying to achieve.

If there's a language barrier, (and I can't stress the importance of this enough) don't leave that call until your workers can describe in their own words what the problem or solution is. You have to take an executive role in the process. They cannot run your company, your roadmap or your vision for you.

Q: What was your outsourcing process? How did you find your programmers and designers?

AppSource

A: They were introduced to us through a friend of my co-founder. The company, Inmite, was personally recommended and I would happily extend that recommendation.

We used them for all initial design and development.

Q: Do you think that app entrepreneurs are at any sort of disadvantage without understanding the basics of iOS programming? How can they mitigate the risk that the programmers they hire may take advantage of this situation?

A: To a certain extent. But they can always learn. It's okay not to have a Computer Science background but if you're investing in making an app then one of two things is true:

1. This is a significant investment for your company and plays a role in your strategy. It's probably worthwhile to buy a book. There are plenty of fundamental iPhone app development books and if you're not experienced at coordinating projects you should read up on that too. My personal strategy in this case is typically to bring in someone you know who is up on this stuff as an adviser. Most people love this title so much they'll do it for free.

2. This isn't a significant investment for your company–then you clearly have enough money to hire someone to oversee the process from your side. Running an outsourced project is pretty much a full time job.

Also–trust your gut. If you don't feel good about a team / someone then just walk away. Be extremely discriminating.

Q: How has *Corkbin* done to date in the App Store since its launch? If this isn't too sensitive for you, do you mind revealing downloads to date?

A: While we can't reveal numbers, we have been pleased with the reception. *Corkbin* was featured in the 'New and Noteworthy' section for several weeks, and has since been in several App Store curated featured app packs.

Q: That's alright. Can you tell us more about how *Corkbin* is monetized though?

A: It originally cost $0.99 to download. It's now free. Users can purchase wine directly through *Corkbin* in our next release and our vision on monetization is around recommendations and sales. We're currently considering raising money to bring more functions in-house so that we can accelerate this process.

Q: What were your biggest challenges and lessons learnt from releasing *Corkbin*? Would you create *Corkbin* today in a different way?

A: Software is easy. Understanding your user is the hard part; creating a product just gets you to the starting line. The biggest challenges that we faced were in understanding users' wants and needs, and adapting to them. And frankly, finding them and telling them about *Corkbin*.

Q: Do you think there's a formula for success on the App Store? If so, what do you think that formula is?

AppSource

A: Sort of. There's a formula for putting your best foot forward and getting a shot. However, there seems to be a lot of randomness thrown in there for good measure.

1. Your app must be useful. It must do something, preferably only one thing, and do it extremely well. Useless Apps go nowhere. Unless it's a game. But that's a whole different world I don't understand.

2. Your app *must* be beautiful. The icon and interface *must* be beautiful. The vast majority of the decision between Apps with similar functionality will be made on this alone.

3. Market it. Apps aren't found by themselves. Issue a press release. If you don't have a lot of money to spend on marketing, use AppLaunch (http://applaunch.us) to get your App to all of the App review sites. Reviews = downloads = features = more downloads.

4. Engage with your users on social media. Quickly fix issues. Issue press-releases / re-AppLaunch for updates and re-releases.

Q: Do you conduct beta-tests with potential users for your apps? If you do, how do you go about it?

A: *TestFlight.* It's an iOS developer's best friend. We have a pilot group now of around 100 users who get all our betas–they're always on a build testing something. Before we were that established, we would tweet, walk into wine shops and offer etc. You do what you have to do to get user feedback.

Chapter: 3

Q: Hey, that's true hustle. It's just part of what you have to do as a smaller developer if you want to succeed. Now that there are more than 900,000 apps on the App Store, do you think that the market is becoming a bit too saturated for the average independent developer to succeed?

A: Well, yes and no. It's definitely a problem that we're starting to see but there are people who are aware of this situation and are focusing on indie developers. It's no longer true that a small developer has the exact same chances as your Rovios and Zyngas, but it's still the most wide-open distribution platform for software. The only difference is, you need to be truly innovative now, whereas a couple of years ago you could essentially launch total rubbish.

Even great apps require press to discovered and that's the reason why I also co-founded AppLaunch (http://applaunch.us) to help indie developers get their apps out through a channel that reviewers listen to, without dropping $3–$10k on retaining a PR firm. We basically run at cost at the moment with the aim of helping to balance the odds towards indie developers a little more. Any monetization beyond cost will always come from the reviewer side.

Q: How do you think independent iPhone app developers can succeed going forward?

A: Work hard and only make software that can be great. You can no longer expect something you make in a weekend to make you a millionaire, so the cost-benefit calculation in your head should be different. You should be asking, 'Is this something that can see returns on 3-6 months of development?'

AppSource

Q: Why do you think most indie developers seem to have such a hard time making a living from selling their apps?

A: Most of them suck. This probably isn't a popular opinion, but there are people making terrible software in all industries and mobile apps are no different. There are, however, definitely groups of developers making great apps that just don't have the time to market and money to invest in their apps. Again, people aren't looking for your app (most of the time)–the majority of apps out there are 'wants' or luxury items so you have to sell them to a user.

Startups exist for a reason. It's a framework around a product to increase the resource (both money and time) that can be spent on an app while minimizing risk to individuals. Angels and VC firms exist for a reason too. Making software of the quality that users of the App Store demand isn't quick or cheap, and frankly, is often beyond the resources of most indie developers. There is a choice–go big or go home.

Be prepared to spend all your time and as much money making your app the best it can be, or accept that you'll be out-marketed, out-innovated and out-executed.

Q: Do you think that as a developer that doesn't code, you're at a distinct disadvantage as independent developers that are programming their own apps are already struggling to survive?

A: Not really. I actually think it proved to be an advantage for my co-founder. You are forced to focus on the most important parts of running any business–product, positioning and revenue. It increases the financial requirements of starting but that's just a

Chapter: 3

reality of not being able to do the work yourself. You can always find a co-founder if you need to.

Q: What words of advice would you have for someone just starting out in iPhone development?

A: Well, here a couple of tips:

1) Development will end up taking three to five times longer than you think.

2) You won't get any downloads on day one unless you market

3) Just because your product/company exists does not make it newsworthy. Make a story, come up with the benefits you offer, and sell (not literally) that story to the press.

4) Have a plan beyond making the app. That is just the beginning of your app adventure.

Q: What online resources would you recommend for app development?

A: I'm a big fan of TestFlight, AppFigures, AppLaunch.us, PRWeb, and Trello.

Q: Do you develop for the iPad? What do you think are the advantages/disadvantages of focusing on the iPad?

AppSource

A: Nope. The iPad is great if you're a content provider, shop or big enough that it's a no-brainer to do it. Otherwise the appeal seems limited for the moment. The utility use-cases haven't been proven yet as it's not a device that people engage with while walking down the street or at a cafe as much as the iPhone. Also, app spending on non-content/ shop apps is significantly lower than on the iPhone.

Q: What's currently your favorite iOS app, and why?

A: Hmm...I guess I'll have to say *Path*...because I'm constantly stealing UI ideas from it! *Netflix* is awesome, and *Trello* is very handy as well.

Q: What is your development setup like? How large is your development team?

A: We have four people in the team. We all use MacBook Air 2012s with 27" Apple Screens. We have a pretty flat structure with individuals taking lead on different projects / features.

Q: Do you do any marketing for your apps, and if so, how do you go about doing it? Do you have any sort of marketing budget?

A: We mostly use AppLaunch.us–we will occasionally run a PRWeb press release for really big announcements but it always hurts the wallet!

Q: Have you done any paid advertising, and if so, have you seen any Return on Investment (ROI) on it?

A: We have experimented with it. Most of it does not return. Google Adwords can be excellent if sensibly used or terrible if not. Focus on maximizing conversions, not Click Through Rates (CTR)!!

Q: It's also been mentioned that a 'Launch Strategy' is becoming increasingly important towards getting eyeballs for apps, with bigger developers paying high amounts per user for the indirect benefit of being seen on the charts.

What are your thoughts on this? Do you think it's an ethical practice?

A: We've never done this. The closest we've come is once participating in a 'Free App A Day' promotion. This isn't too different and had a big effect. Ultimately, people will do whatever they can to stay competitive; this is all really due to the fact that the App Store has terrible discovery mechanisms and terrible App recommendations. I wouldn't do it, but I find it hard to blame people who do.

Q: The buzzword for a while now in the app developer scene is Freemium. Do you think that pursuing this strategy will continue to be feasible over the long haul? What are your thoughts on how app monetization will change in the future?

A: 'Freemium' is as much a buzzword as 'Sale'. While it's only been coined recently, the concept of giving somebody something for free and using it as bait to entice them to pay you for something more has been around for a long time.

AppSource

It makes good sense, when it makes good sense. However, as with all buzzwordy concepts, it is misused by companies that don't understand that:

- A trial does not make a Freemium product
- The free part has to be useful in some way

The idea is that you can have a thriving community of users who actually actively use your free product to some sort of effect and may never need to upgrade, with another group of users who require the premium feature-set who do upgrade. Free users become evangelists and attract other free users–there will be some rate of conversion from free to premium. 5% suggests a healthy Freemium model. Evernote is a great example of this.

Q: I guess we'll end on that note. Thanks so much for taking the time out to do this interview.

A: My pleasure.

Chapter 4

Jon Stinson

◆

How A Music Producer Outsources iOS Games On The Side

While Jon Stinson makes a living in the music industry as a freelance producer / recordist / balance engineer, he likes to identify himself as an opportunity seeker. Originally interested in developing music-related apps, he put his ideas on the backburner for three to four years thinking that it'd cost him too much to get started.

After attending a marketing seminar in San Diego, Jon came to realize that it was possible to outsource the development of an app for substantially cheaper than what he originally imagined.

With this in mind, he made the decision to consciously immerse himself in developing iPhone apps on the side. His app development startup, Curious Idea, has since released the iPhone games *Syntax Match* and *Best Zombies Detector Scanner*.

***

Q: Could you please tell us a little about your background and how you got into iPhone app development?

AppSource

A: My background is actually in the music business. I'm a freelance record producer, recording engineer, and mixing engineer out of Nashville, TN. I've always been interested in many different forms of technology, though and although I've never really been particularly gifted at writing code, or understanding the more sophisticated "under the hood" aspects of computer technology, it's always been something that has interested me.

As an early teenager, I would geek out with my cousin about computers. His was a PC -back then we just called them IBM machines–and mine was a Mac. We always debated which was the better platform. This was back before Microsoft made Windows, so all his computer did was run DOS. I couldn't wrap my mind around the blank black screen. To me, clearly Apple machines were better!

During these early teenage years, I toyed around with the idea of creating programs on the Mac, yet never really put forth any effort to learn anything, as my foremost passion was in making music. Later as an adult, I became interested in developing iPhone apps, once that new technology came to market.

Late last year, I got an email from a marketer talking about how he had been creating games on the iPhone. His focus was on the marketing side of the equation, and it all made a lot of sense to me. He was selling an information course, and I decided to go for it, finally acting on my interests in developing programs on an Apple platform.

Q: From what I understand, you outsource the entire programming and design aspect of all your apps. Have you had any difficulties in communicating exactly what you wanted while doing so?

A: Yes, I do indeed outsource everything. This is one of the biggest aspects of the business that I'm building, and pretty much the main reason that it's possible for me to be able to create iPhone apps. The rise of the outsourcing websites in the last few years is a key movement in modern day business.

For several years before I started making apps, I heard people talk about how they were outsourcing a good bit of their work to these freelance sites, but I was very skeptical of it all. Once I was visually walked through the process of what it looked like to post a job, interview for a job, and hire for a job on these sites, I immediately understood the hype. Now I'm thrilled that these services exist, and use them for all my projects.

As far as the communication goes, I haven't run into too many difficulties, but I believe that's because I was shown how to work the hiring process when using these sites. Basically the key is to exercise the 'slow to hire and quick to fire' method. You have to spend a lot of time going through applicants and paying attention to detail on their job postings.

Q: 'Slow to hire and quick to fire' seems to be somewhat of a mantra amongst the app entrepreneurs I've spoken to so far but do go on...

A: Haha. That's probably because it's a good mantra to adopt if you want to remain in business!

Well, so once you've narrowed it down to a few select candidates, interview them on Skype to see what their communication skills are like, as well as their ability to understand and pick up on the concepts you are describing. How fluent are they in English? They don't *have* to speak English flawlessly – even though most of

AppSource

them do – but you have to decide what your threshold is, so that there's less risk of fundamental breakdowns in communication.

When describing the process of working remotely via the freelance sites, it sounds very arduous. In reality, while the initial hiring process is fairly tedious, the day-to-day management of the project is pretty straightforward. It's important that you spend time putting the work in on the hiring process though. If you don't get that right, then chances are you will end up with a contractor who is an impediment to the project. It's not uncommon for me to go through up to five rounds of job postings for a project before I find someone that I want to hire.

Q: Do you think that you're at any sort of disadvantage without understanding the basics of iOS programming?

A: Not at all. While I do plan to familiarize myself a bit more with iOS programming at some point in the future, I don't think I'm at a disadvantage because I'm not able to write my own code or completely understand what I'm looking at when I see it. I know what I want out of an app, and I know how to direct people to build it. If programmers can't deliver what I want without speaking in technical terms, then things just aren't going to work.

Q: Even if you don't think it's a disadvantage, how do you mitigate the risk that the programmers you hire might possibly take advantage of this situation?

A: If programmers attempt to exploit my inability to write and/or read code, then they're not going to be working with me. I might not be one hundred percent familiar with all the technical aspects of everything involving creating a mobile app, but I'm not ignorant either. I know when things aren't right, and it doesn't take long to figure out that someone is trying to take advantage of you.

Q: If you don't mind sharing, how successful has your app been to date in terms of sales/downloads?

A: No, I don't mind sharing at all. To date I have had just over 20,000 downloads of my app *Syntax Match*. *Best Zombies Detector Scanner* has not had anywhere near that many downloads, but I've also not fully implemented my marketing plan for it yet.

Q: Did you expect your app to be as successful as it is? Why do you think it became so successful, and what do you think you did right with it?

A: As this was my first run in the app world, I really didn't know what to expect in terms of downloads. Honestly, one of the key reasons *Syntax Match* was successful was because of a promotion I did with an app promotion company that has an active audience. The other thing I did right was basing my game on a model that has been proven to be successful. It's a type of game people want to play.

Also, creating a game with high quality graphics, sounds, and user experience is very important in getting downloads and keeping people interested in playing your game.

Q: I guess with the increased competition in the App Store, a polished game is probably a given if you want to even stand a chance of hitting the charts! Do you think there's a formula for success in the App Store? If so, what do you think that formula is?

AppSource

A: I don't think there really is a formula to being successful in anything in life, besides hard work and perseverance. That being said, there is a playbook, per se, of key things that are repeatable and put developers in a position to put their best foot forward, and get some traction with their apps.

In the app and the mobile marketplace, trends change very quickly – on a near daily basis. For example, nine months to a year ago, making your app free to download with In-App-Purchases (IAPs) was a very lucrative tactic. Now, however, people are not buying these IAPs nearly as much, and developers are relying more on ads as a monetization strategy.

Outside of this, tactics such as establishing relationships with other developers and trading traffic with them, buying traffic from some of the better promotional services, integrating pop-ups within the game that ask people to rate your game, maintaining good customer support, using push notifications to bring people back into your app, and consistently building and expanding your network of apps are all examples of small and simple, yet effective tactics to employ when attempting to get people to download and continually use your apps.

Q: Yup, and that sort of ties in with what you were saying earlier about how your partnership with an app promotion company played a large part in the success of *Syntax Match*. What were the biggest challenges and lessons learnt from releasing your app? Would you create the same app today in a different way?

A: I learned two significant lessons through the process of developing and releasing it. The first lesson I learned, is how important it is to run a tight ship in terms of the team you build and work with.

Again, the key phrase is "be slow to hire, and quick to fire." When developing an app, things can get complicated very quickly. It's a complicated process to develop an app, and keep everything on time and within budget. The slightest issue can cause your development time to fall way behind, which can cause it to cost a lot more money. So, it's important to fix the cause of the issue right away, whatever that might be.

The second lesson I learned is how important it is to use an app name that is descriptive and utilizes keywords. Clever and interesting names can be cool, artistic, fun and inspiring, but often times can cause your app to disappear into oblivion, as it more than likely incorporates words that no one is searching for. "Syntax" is just not a word people are searching for on the App Store.

If I was going to do it over again, I would make the same app, but I would make some different choices regarding the branding and the name. I also wouldn't have made the app nearly as detailed from the start. Currently, there are four game modes to choose from in *Syntax Match*. I would have only one mode, and not done any IAPs. These more built out features, I would have included in updates. For *Best Zombies Detector Scanner*, I incorporated these learning experiences into the development process, and was able to keep things simpler, keep the development time shorter, and keep development costs lower. (*Best Zombies Detector Scanner* cost about 75% less to make).

Q: Do you conduct beta-tests with potential users for your apps? If you do, how do you go about it?

A: So far, I have not conducted any type of beta testing program when building apps. The method I've gone about employing, is

AppSource

to use a simple provisioning service called 'Test Flight' that allows my programmer to send me an email with a link to download and install test builds of my app throughout different stages in the development process.

There are a couple of other developers I'm close to who I will loop in with this 'Test Flight' provisioning access, so that they can provide third party feedback. But as far as opening up to a semi-public beta testing group, I find it's much more simple to just go ahead and release the app in the market place, and listen to user feedback there. Then, we simply do an update, which takes into account the revisions and features people asked for the most.

Q: Now that there are close to 900,000 apps on the app store, do you think that the market is becoming too saturated?

A: I actually think the market became saturated a long time ago. But it's like anything else. Work really hard to make great and remarkable products (what Seth Godin refers to as a purple cow). Doing remarkable work is always worth doing. Besides, I come from a music production background, so I don't think you can get more saturated than that. Plenty of hit songs have already been written, but that does not mean that there won't continue to be hits.

Q: So true. How do you think independent iPhone developers can succeed going forward?

A: Continue to pay attention to the trends. Stay connected. Keep establishing and maintaining high quality relationships with other developers. Do remarkable work. Keep on learning. Don't just constantly look for shortcuts but be diligent in running a legitimate business, while thinking long term. Don't treat app development like the newest, hottest thing to get rich and famous from. Think about how to create meaning, build a business, and make a profit over the long term.

Q: **What words of advice would you have for someone just starting out in iPhone development?**

A: Making iPhone apps is worth doing if you really want to do it. But just keep your expectations in check. If you're approaching this as a 'get rich quick' scheme, it's not going to work. 'Get rich quick' is not a viable business model. So understand that it takes a lot of hard work to get traction, and to get your apps to the top of the charts. The goal should be sustainable income, and it takes hard work and daily upkeep to get there.

Another piece of advice I could share is to focus on what makes money, which in the App Store, is games by a long shot. It's fine to do other types of apps from time to time, but games are the most downloaded apps of any category on the App Store. They are also the easiest to monetize. Whatever you do, keep it simple, and always try to improve on a proven concept that has been shown to work in the marketplace – don't try to re-invent the wheel.

Q: **Do you develop for the iPad? What do you think are the advantages / disadvantages of focusing on the iPad?**

A: So far I have yet to develop any apps that are specific to the iPad. The reason is because there are not nearly as many iPads in the market as there are iPhones. So the development cost to profit ratio is too much of a spread to make financial sense. And since

AppSource

iPhone apps will also run on an iPad, it just makes the most sense to focus on the iPhone. You get the most bang for your buck this way.

Q: What's currently your favorite iOS app, and why?

A: Haha, great question. I definitely like many of the games that have come to be household names, such as *Angry birds*, *Temple Run*, and *Bejeweled* (which is what *Syntax Match* is based on), but there are also some games that are pretty popular, but not quite as ubiquitous as the aforementioned selections that I really love. Some of these favorites include *Crystal Crusher*, *100 Floors*, *Whale Trail*, and *Robot Unicorn Attack*.

Q: What is your development setup like? How large is your development team?

A: My development setup is really simple. Right now my team consists of two programmers and one designer. I'm currently in the process of hiring another designer. On the technical end, I do all my work from my Macbook Pro. It's simple but it's always better not to overcomplicate things.

Q: Do you do any marketing for your apps, and if so how do you go about doing it? Do you have any sort of marketing budget?

A: I most definitely do! This consists of everything from cross promotion in my own network, to buying traffic through promotional services. As far as my marketing budget, it depends on what I'm trying to do with the app (serve as a feeder app, or more a primary app), and what the Revenue Per Install (RPI) is.

Q: Have you found success with buying traffic and if so, have you seen any ROI on it?

A: I did see a return on it, although it was not as much as I had hoped it would be. My spike in downloads caused me to pull in some good money through the ads I run in *Syntax Match*. Moving forward, the goal is to grow my network so that promotions such as this are more impactful.

Q: What metrics do you use to gauge success, and what resources do you use for this?

A: Well, I would say that pretty much all the metrics I pay attention to would be online metrics, the biggest one being my eCPM. Next would be my total daily downloads, the daily and monthly ad impressions delivered, the daily and monthly installs I've driven via the ads, the daily and monthly bootups, the number of monthly sessions, and conversions on certain things like IAPs and power ups (if my app offers them as *Syntax Match* does).

Q: It's also been mentioned that a 'Launch Strategy' is becoming increasingly important towards getting eyeballs for apps, with bigger developers paying high amounts per user for the indirect benefit of being seen on the charts. What are your thoughts on this? Do you think it's an ethical practice?

A: As long as you are getting your downloads in an honest way, I see no ethical issue. I am aware that some promotional services have

AppSource

come into question as to how exactly they get you downloads, but I don't do business with anyone who is questionable. Apple is also very aggressive in maintaining their brand, so anyone who is using unethical practices to get downloads will be eradicated pretty quickly.

I do think it is important to think about and consider what your options are as far as a launch strategy goes when releasing an app. I don't think that it's smart to do this by default every time you put an app out. You have to consider what purpose you're targeting by putting the app out. Are you trying to expand your network of apps by releasing a feeder app? Or are you intending to put out a new "flagship" app? If it's a feeder app, then don't waste the money on a launch promotion. If it's a "flagship" app, then it's probably worth planning a launch. The number one promotional tool for an app are the App Store charts. Spending a substantial amount of money to buy traffic and push your app up the charts is a viable strategy.

Q: How important do you think constant updates are in retaining users and maintaining downloads?

A: Constant updates are very important. It's part of the whole customer service end of the business. You need to provide a high quality customer experience on all fronts – from the quality of your game, to the support you offer. Monitoring what your customer base wants and giving it to them is part of providing that support. It shows that you care about what you are doing, that you aren't just pushing out apps and moving on, but that you are constantly improving and refining your apps.

Q: What are your thoughts on the recent revelation that Apple is clamping down on app store rankings manipulation from bots and human armies?

A: This goes back to the question on ethics. Like I said, Apple is protecting their brand. They want to guarantee a certain experience to people, and a certain amount of 'policing' is involved in this process. Sometimes I do think Apple is a little heavy handed in their control of the marketplace, but I totally support their decision to eradicate bots from the App Store.

Honestly, even if Apple didn't do this, it would not be a viable business model. Anytime you attempt to 'game' the system (excuse the pun), it's a race to the bottom. While there might exist shortcuts throughout the life of an industry, the way you're really and truly going to win with people is providing something they can truly trust in. Now, that's a long-term strategy.

Q: What do you think is the best way to drive downloads over time?

A: It's basically the cumulative effort of everything I've already mentioned and working hard at it day after day over the long term. In a nutshell:

- Focus on games, as they get the most downloads.

- Improve upon concepts that have already been proven to work – don't try to re-invent the wheel.

- Create high quality games, apps and user experiences.

- Provide great support.

AppSource

- Build your network of apps – the more apps you have out, the greater your reach. The greater your reach, the more effectively you can cross promote your apps.

Q: Awesome. We've come to the end of the interview. Thanks for the summation and for the interview as well.

A: You're welcome. Thanks for having me.

Chapter 5

Petr Fodor

◆

Quitting A Lucrative Job In Advertising To Develop *Power Of Logic*

After suffering from mild burn-out at work, Petr Fodor decided to quit a lucrative job in advertising when he recognized the enormous potential in the mobile gaming market. Joining forces with a fellow colleague, Petr co-founded the app development company, Flow Studio Games.

A self-proclaimed business mechanic, Petr has outsourced the development of his games to freelancers from all around the world. Despite not having any previous experience in programming or developing apps, Petr and his co-founder found that their previous working experience made it easier for them to find the correct local partners in making their first game, *Power of Logic*, a success.

Since then, Flow Studio Games has started working with Techsquare, a start-up accelerator based in Prague, Czech Republic and recently released their second game, *Sortee*.

***

Q: Could you please tell us a little about your background and how you got involved with iPhone app development?

AppSource

A: I spent ten years working in advertising. Such a job makes you tired after working for such a long time. My colleague Richard and I realized that we were spending too much time doing something we weren't passionate about anymore and that's why we decided to make such a big switch.

This also had something to do with the massive growth in the mobile gaming market as well. We quit the agency, where we had very lucrative jobs, and stepped out into uncertainty. We do what we love and we give it 100 percent of our all. We used to look forward to the weekend, now we look forward to starting work on Monday.

Q: That's very inspiring. From what I understand, you outsource the entire programming and design aspect of all your apps. Have you had any difficulties in communicating exactly what you wanted while doing so?

A: Definitely, this happens all the time. It's one aspect that you can't avoid when the entire team isn't sitting in one office. In fact, we don't have any problems with the results but how we get to them in the first place. Although we are used to working with freelancers, misunderstandings still crop up from time to time. What helps is to write down a detailed brief, to follow up often and to set an open atmosphere where no one is afraid to ask anything.

Q: How necessary do you think an NDA is for someone outsourcing development of an app?

A: Generally we have a rule to have a written deal with key members of the team. It is valuable for both sides because we set out rules, responsibilities, payments and sanctions. Having an NDA for secrecy's sake is unnecessary because the idea itself counts for very little. Everyone has a 'great' idea. Execution is what matters most in any entrepreneurial pursuit.

Q: Agreed. Considering that both you and your partner Richard didn't have any experience in game development, what made you want to develop games for iOS in the first place?

A: Firstly, we thought there was potential in this market and secondly, both of us have endless creativity and space for designing our own products. The responsibility for the output and success is absolutely thrilling for us! We love when people enjoy spending their time with something we have created.

Q: How has *Power of Logic* done to date in the App Store in terms of sales/downloads?

A: We have almost 800,000 downloads so far and two basic ways of monetization. First is Pay Per Download and the second is advertising provided by Chartboost. The revenue proportion is now 2:1.

Q: Wow, 800,000 downloads is no mean feat. However, do you think that you're at any sort of disadvantage in this business without understanding the basics of iOS programming? How do you mitigate the risk that the programmers you hire might possibly take advantage of this situation?

A: By choosing the right people whom we can trust. Game development is a long and painful process, and relationships need to be strong. We always want to set the motivations for our freelancers to have some sort of stake in the company's success even if the work is only for hire. You can motivate people with profit sharing, bonuses for reaching milestone within a set time, and so on.

Q: Did you expect *Power of Logic* to be as successful as it was? What do you think you did right with the app and why?

A: We actually expected *Power of Logic* to earn us more money soon after the launch. More of its success came after we closed a sponsorship deal with T-Mobile and discovered new revenue streams from advertising. Anyway the main goal was to learn about development and marketing which was incredibly useful.

I think there are two main reasons why we can consider the game a success:

1. We are not programmers—we have designed the game from the very beginning as a product, which needs to be sold. We chose a classic concept, set a narrow target audience of hard-core logic players, created an interesting game environment and hired one of the best graphic designers.

2. We had a Plan B and C in case our launch was a failure. Regardless of how hard we worked on the launch, we had plans on what to do in case we didn't reach clearly defined sales targets as expected. This helped us to find a local partner early and later to discover alternative revenue streams from advertising. This means we have 'milked the marketing cow' as much as possible.

Q: If you were starting out in iPhone app development again, what would you do differently?

A: I'd be absolutely certain that my idea was unique. You'll be spending lots of time and paying off various contractors so confidence is essential. I'd share my ideas, mockups and demos with as many people as possible.

As mentioned earlier, it's a waste of time to be concerned with whether someone will steal the idea. With *Sortee*, we managed to get valuable feedback from the very beginning, which was something we missed out on with *Power of Logic*.

Something I'd also have done differently would be to hire a designer and programmer full-time from the start. We were delayed for months with the game development at the beginning just because we chose a programmer who was working on another game simultaneously!

Q: Do you think there's a formula for success in the App Store? If so, what do you think that formula is?

A: I don't know if there's a formula but a simple guideline would be to have a unique and totally polished product.

Q: What were your biggest challenges and lessons learnt from releasing your first app?

A: There were so many lessons learnt I don't know where to start! I'll just mention one of the most important ones–test your future colleagues! CVs and portfolios aren't enough. Interviews and polite answers are not enough. Test real skills on real briefs with

AppSource

real outputs and real deadlines. This will tell you much more about the candidate and will save you an unbelievable amount of time and money.

Q: Do you have a process for going from app idea to full-blown development?

A: Yes, we have two steps pre-production:

The game idea is captured in a one-page template where the author describes basic mechanics, design style, pros and cons, etc.

We then create detailed sketches of the game and a game development document that we use to cover the game from the basics to the finer details, such as how we animate screens and what text appears on the player's Facebook wall when the player shares his high score.

Q: Do you conduct beta-tests with potential users for your apps? If you do, how do you go about it?

A: We test the game with early prototypes. At first, we only use our partners and friends. We just let them play and watch what they do without any interruptions. When we progress further, we have at least three external testers who get a testing screenplay and form on how to capture bugs. For our latest game *Sortee*, we also had a third round of testing with the general public.

Q: Now that there are more than 900,000 apps on the app store, do you think that the market is becoming too saturated for the average independent developer to succeed?

A: Well, that depends. Who is the average indie developer? I'm sure there's always enough space for great applications and games. The market is currently extremely competitive but I think you can still become a success when you work really hard and think carefully about your next steps.

Q: How do you think independent iPhone developers can succeed going forward?

A: Spend your time analyzing the featured applications and games for inspiration, follow relevant journalists and talk to people who have already succeeded. Do your best and hope it will be enough. If not, well…at least you'll be getting bucket loads of experience that'll come into play for your next app.

Q: Well, as the saying goes, experience is the best teacher. Why do you think most indie developers seem to have such a hard time making a living from selling their own apps?

A: Because most of us are fighting big production houses and the average consumer doesn't know the difference between 'Indie' and 'Commercial' products. If indies wants to get attention, their apps must at least be of similar quality to the titles published by the big players.

Q: What words of advice would you have for someone just starting out in iPhone app development?

A: Concentrate on a market niche. The App Store is huge and the smallest market segment is still big enough to earn you a lot of money. Create something unique and get confirmation from at least 10 experts that it is truly unique. Hire only the very best people for your team and motivate them well.

Q: Aside from Chartboost which you mentioned earlier, do you use any other online resources for app development?

A: We use Test Flight, App Annie, Distimo, Flurry, MobileDevHQ, Promoter. We also plan to use Redeemco.de from our friends Tappy Taps before the launch of our future apps.

Q: What do you think are the advantages/disadvantages of focusing on the iPad?

A: The big advantages are the higher monetization per user and the additional space to play with. The big disadvantage would be the significantly smaller number of iPads out there relative to iPhones.

Q: What is your development setup like? How large is your development team?

A: We have two teams working on two separate apps for a while:

Sortee had one designer and one programmer and we added a second programmer to speed up the development.

StyleBee has one designer, an Android/backend programmer and two iOS programmers.

Richard is head of *Sortee* and I lead the *StyleBee* team.

Q: How do you go about marketing your apps?

A: Heh, we could probably write a book about the topic! Briefly, we spent a lot of time marketing our apps using App Store optimization, trailers, PR, viral campaigns, etc.

Q: Did you do any paid advertising, and if so, have you seen any ROI on it?

A: We haven't done any paid advertising so far but we plan to try Facebook ads for *StyleBee* because it matches our target group behavior very well.

Q: The buzzword for a while now in the app developer scene is 'Freemium'. Do you think that pursuing this strategy will continue to be feasible over the long haul? What are your thoughts on how app monetization will change in the future?

A: I have a very simple answer using today's *Power of Logic* figures in Flurry: *Power of Logic* had ten illegal downloads to one paid for last week. Freemium can help us to get at least part of the money we are missing out on now. However, the model has to be fair, well implemented in games mechanics and generous to players.

Q: What are your thoughts on cross promotion?

A: It's definitely useful. We plan cross promotions with a few selected partners who have similar target audiences and good products.

AppSource

Q: How important do you think constant updates are in retaining users and maintaining downloads?

A: Frankly, we don't have enough experience to answer this question. I think it depends a lot on the game/app concept and if you can deliver interesting additional content over the long term.

Q: Ok, one final question before we wrap things up. What are your thoughts on the recent revelation that Apple is clamping down on app store rankings manipulation from bots and human armies?

A: Thank God. Finally! While they're at it, they should also improve the App Store search engine!

Q: I guess we'll end on that note. Thanks for taking the time out for this interview!

A: It's been a pleasure.

Chapter 6
Austin L. Church

◆

From Getting Laid Off To Building A Successful App Development Company

Austin L. Church didn't get into the app business by choice. During the recession of 2009, he was laid off from the marketing firm he was working in and propelled headfirst into the realm of self-employment. He started freelancing, and joined a Mastermind group to grow his newly founded marketing business. However, the group buzz seemed to revolve around building mobile applications, and before long, Austin was hooked.

A few months later, after some intensive research and story boarding, *Mustache Bash* was born, becoming a bona fide hit in the App Store with over 270,000 downloads to date. Buoyed by this success, Austin went on to develop more apps, the likes of which include *Cheap Shot Insults Shaker*, *Crazy Alarm Clock* and *Whamsy Sound Bombs*. If the whimsical nature of his existing apps are anything to go by, we can probably expect many more quirky entertainment apps to come.

Today, Austin is the brains behind Bright Newt, the same company he founded for his freelance marketing services. Coupled with his newfound skill sets, he has expanded his business line to include mobile app consulting as well.

***

AppSource

Q: Hi Austin. Shall we start off with you telling us about your background and how you got into iPhone app development?

A: My background is in English education. I taught high school for a year before moving to Knoxville, Tennessee, to earn my Master of Arts (MA) in English. I never wanted to be a businessman; I thought I was going to be an English professor! After finishing my Master's degree, I got a job at a marketing firm, but after about six months, I started freelancing.

In June 2011 I joined a Mastermind group to help grow my marketing business, but all everyone seemed to be talking about was mobile apps. I caught the bug and started researching how to build my first app, *Mustache Bash*.

Q: Has your background in marketing helped you in getting the word out on *Mustache Bash*? If so, can you tell us more about it?

A: Yes, my marketing background has been a huge help. The business world is not a meritocracy, and neither is the App Store. Lots of great apps never get found because their developers believe in the *Field of Dreams* fallacy: if you build it, they will come.

Q: From what I understand, you outsourced the entire programming and design aspect of *Mustache Bash*. Have you had any difficulties in communicating exactly what you wanted to do while doing so?

A: Of course! Things are always getting lost in translation. It's not until you try to communicate with someone whose native language is one other than English that you realize how nuanced and complex language is.

How do you explain the following to a designer: "That button is too spiky. It's too much like the starburst callouts you see on everything. I want something fresher, something more distinctive." It takes twice as many words, and you still don't get your point across sometimes. You've got to be persistent though.

App development has too many tasks, to-dos, and decisions. You have to choose your compromises very carefully, or you'll really damage the app's overall quality. That being said, I've been blessed to find and collaborate with some amazing designers and coders. Any communication issues were totally worth it.

Q: What was your outsourcing process? How did you find your programmers and designers?

A: I've found programmers and designers on oDesk and Freelancer. Elance, Vworker, and Guru offer similar services. My process was fairly straightforward: hire slowly and fire quickly. I look for talent, obviously, and attention to detail. I want someone who is conscientious and thorough. I never reveal much about the project in the posting, and I always interview people in a Skype chat.

I've got a list of interview questions that help me hire based on qualifications rather than personality. Though I prefer to work with people I like, I've found that the people who are best at selling themselves are often the ones who struggle to follow through. At the end of the day, I've got a business to run, and I need my contractors to deliver on time and within budget.

AppSource

> Establish expectations up front, and then you have a measuring stick to gauge someone's performance and integrity.

Q: Do you think that you're at any sort of disadvantage without understanding the basics of iOS programming? How do you mitigate the risk that the programmers you hire might possibly take advantage of this situation?

A: There's always the risk that a programmer will use my ignorance to fatten up his bank account. But I've found that people show their true colors rather quickly. People with nothing to hide don't mind a long interview. Judging someone's character isn't difficult if you know what to look for. I ask for references and contact those past clients. I ask programmers to send builds to Assembla so that I always have a copy of what I'm paying for. I start contracts with a series of small tests and deadlines in order to evaluate a contractor's willingness to work on my terms. I also break down projects into individual tasks and ask for an hourly estimate on each task. I know enough developers now who would be able to tell me whether those hourly estimates are reasonable.

Q: How has *Mustache Bash* done to date in the App Store since its launch in April? Has it been profitable thus far? If this isn't too sensitive for you, do you mind revealing downloads / sales to date?

A: *Mustache Bash* has had over 270,000 downloads. Unfortunately, I left a lot of money on the table because I didn't employ certain advanced monetization strategies out of the gate–you live and learn, right? *Mustache Bash* has paid for itself. Having a successful app in the App Store is a strong form of credibility that I have also been able to leverage for several consulting gigs.

Q: That's interesting. How did you manage to leverage *Mustache Bash* into consulting gigs?

A: Having an app in the App Store is really the only form of credibility you need. As with any other business, there are people out there who want somebody else to do everything for them. I have been talking a lot about iOS development on Facebook and Twitter quite a bit, so people have begun to see me as an expert. When they have questions or are looking for someone to hire, they already know how to get in touch.

Q: What were your biggest challenges and lessons learnt from releasing *Mustache Bash*?

A: I wouldn't change much about the design or UI, but I would have included banner ads and nag screens in the first release. Otherwise, I'm satisfied with how things have progressed. I knew my first app was going to be an education, and though *Mustache Bash* hasn't been a winning lottery ticket, it has exceeded my expectations.

Q: Ok, let's put it this way. If you were starting out in iPhone app development again, what would you do differently?

A: If I had it to do all over again, I'd shoot for a very, very simple app that would cost less than five hundred dollars to develop. I would build six to eight of these as quickly as possible and save the more expensive, more complex ideas until I'd learned the ropes. But then again, learning the ropes is what taught me what I would do differently!

AppSource

Q: Haha, seems like a chicken and egg kind of situation. Do you think there's a formula for success in the App Store? If so, what do you think that formula is?

A: If there's a formula to success in the App Store, it's related to building a network of apps, knowing your numbers, constantly tweaking monetization, and participating in a community of app developers.

No one does well in isolation. Also, you've got to plan on doing this full-time. Most part-time developers make less than a thousand a month.

Q: Do you have a process for going from app idea to full-blown development?

A: Yes. Research, storyboarding and then Thoreau's maxim: 'Simplify. Simplify. Simplify.'

Q: That's a great maxim for app development. Leave out the overly complicated features and just do one or two things really well.

Do you conduct beta-tests with potential users for your apps? If you do, how do you go about it?

A: Yes. I use TestFlight to distribute ad hoc builds. My wife is one of my best beta testers. Another good tactic is handing my iPhone to a friend and saying, "Play with this app and tell me what you think."

Chapter: 6

> I do NOT tell them that it's mine because I get a more honest opinion that way.

Q: I'm using TestFlight as well and I'm just amazed that it's being offered for free at the moment.

Now that there are more than 900,000 apps on the App Store, do you think that the market is becoming too saturated for the average independent developer to succeed?

A: Yes, if you're the average independent developer who doesn't educate himself about smart marketing and monetization. No, if you're the above-average developer who understands that most of the work begins *after* your app is live in the App Store. The app business is a marathon, not a sprint.

Q: How do you think independent iPhone developers can succeed going forward?

A: By building networks of apps–a herd of milk cows–and then leveraging that existing fan base to more or less guarantee the success of each new app.

Q: Why do you think most indie developers seem to have such a hard time making a living from selling their own apps?

A: Because they don't use the right business model. You can build second-rate games and apps and still be very, very successful if you have the right business model. I personally don't create anything that I don't enjoy using but most indie developers focus on the code, the design or the user experience and totally ignore the most important piece of the puzzle–the business model that holds everything together.

Most indie developers are artists and suffer from the same weakness as other artists trying to make it in the business world–a lack of business acumen.

Q: That's unfortunate but oh so true. I've come across a small number of developers who think it's beneath them to market their apps. It's the 'starving artist' syndrome.

That said, as a developer who doesn't code, do you think you're losing out to someone who programs his own apps?

A: Absolutely not! Rather, I think I have a clear advantage.

Because I don't code or design, I am free to focus on building the business, identifying new opportunities, and generating cashflow.

Q: What words of advice would you have for someone just starting out in iPhone development?

A: K.I.S.S–Keep it simple stupid. Focus on proven, not original, app concepts. Keep your apps as simple as possible. Improve them in phases with new releases based on customer feedback. It's too risky to try to execute an original idea AND find a market for it at the same time. It's less risky to find a hungry crowd and give them a better hamburger.

Q: I like to think both schools of thought have their place in the market. I agree that marketing an original idea would probably be riskier but an original idea that connects with the market would probably have an easier time going viral. Something novel and fresh would probably also have a much easier time getting features and reviews from popular media.

What online resources do you use for app development? Anything you'd like to recommend developers?

A: There are too many to list here. I've already mentioned oDesk and Freelancer. I use AppAnnie, AppFigures, and Flurry for analytics and tracking. Apsalar is another winner. Chomp is useful, as is Top App Charts.

The best resource of all is the App Store itself. It tells you which apps are succeeding all day, every day.

Q: Do you develop for the iPad? What do you think are the advantages/disadvantages of focusing on the iPad?

A: I don't currently develop for iPad, but I plan to. The disadvantages are reworking the iPhone UI to accommodate for the iPad's different aspect ratios. This requires creating two more sets of design assets (standard and retina display). The larger screen size means that you have more real estate, which has pros and cons.

You can put more 'stuff' on the screen, but you also don't want to clutter an otherwise nice UI. However, the advantages definitely outweigh the disadvantages. If I develop for iPad, I'm reaching a larger market.

AppSource

Q: What's currently your favorite iOS app, and why?

A: I love *Skype*. I can text with people all over the world, no matter where I am.

Q: What is your development setup like? How large is your development team?

A: I have four developers. All of them work part-time and remotely. I use Basecamp, email, and Skype to keep everyone on track.

Q: Hmmm, why do you use 4 part-time developers and not stick to 1 full-time guy?

A: Because all my developers are managing other gigs simultaneously. It's hard to find a developer who is talented, affordable, and just so happens to be looking for a full-time gig.

Q: I can imagine. Good technical talent has become so scarce in the startup and app development scene.

Do you do any marketing for your apps, and if so, how do you go about doing it?

A: Most of my marketing has to do with attracting and taking advantage of free exposure. All my profits are going back into development right now, but within a couple of months, I'll be in a place where I can start paying for more traffic.

Chapter: 6

Q: What do you mean by taking advantage of free exposure?

A: Writing lots and lots of emails and networking. Reaching out to people on Twitter. That kind of stuff.

Q: You mention that you're also thinking of paying for traffic...

A: Yup. Even though I haven't done it, plenty of my developer friends have. They see it as an essential part of a smart marketing strategy.

Q: Interesting. You mentioned earlier that you left a lot of money on the table because you didn't employ advanced monetization strategies out the gate. Can you elaborate on this? What kind of monetization strategies are you talking about?

A: There were so many things I left out at the beginning. I would have utilized different types of ads, smarter incorporation of available in-app purchases in the UI, and used affiliate links from iTunes affiliate companies like TradeDoubler and Linkshare.

Q: How important do you think constant updates are for a successful app?

A: Very important. They're a part of the overall marketing strategy and help keep an app fresh and spur user engagement.

**Q: It's been mentioned that a 'Launch Strategy' is becoming increasingly important towards getting eyeballs for apps, with bigger developers paying high amounts per user for the indirect benefit of being seen on the charts.

What are your thoughts on this? Do you think it's an ethical practice?

A: I don't think it's unethical because it's no different from buying Superbowl airtime. Will you always see certain businesses spending money to try to make money off of crap? Of course. But crappy apps don't have staying power, so these people are wasting their money.

They'll get short-term exposure, but their apps won't be around in six months. With regards to a launch strategy, this is crucial for any kind of business, not just app development companies!

Q: The buzzword for a while now in the app developer scene is 'Freemium'. Do you think that pursuing this strategy will continue to be feasible over the long haul? What are your thoughts on how app monetization will change in the future?

A: Yes, it will continue to be feasible. In the future, I think we will see more digital/physical crossover. Companies will incentivize and reward accomplishments with real goods, whether that be gift cards or cash or a free coffee somewhere.

Digital goods aren't going to get less popular, so it stands to reason that more and more organizations will use the digital space to sell or give away physical products.

Chapter: 6

Q: That sounds plausible enough. Anyway, we've come to the end of the interview. Thanks for taking the time out to do this!

A: My pleasure.

Chapter 7
Matt Geoffrey

◆

Making $1.6 Million In App Profits After Nine Months

Matt Geoffrey has had an interesting career, going from selling high-end business intelligence services to Fortune 500 companies, to running an internet marketing company to developing mobile apps for large-scale clients. In his own words, he's a serial internet entrepreneur with several successful business lines.

However, the constant traveling for business took its toll on him, and in 2011, he decided to switch his focus to building his own apps. Despite creating a number of apps that failed commercially at the beginning, Matt persevered and continued to forge ahead when most developers would have simply given up. This paid off in spades when he eventually managed to rake in $1.6 million in profits after just 9 months!

Aside from running his app business, App Networx LLC, he has also decided to 'pay it forward', sharing what he's learnt regarding app monetization so that other developers can do better with their apps. Does this sound too good to be true? Well, you'll just have to read the interview and decide for yourself…

***

Chapter: 7

Q: Hey Matt. Can you tell us about your background and how you got into iPhone app development?

A: Sure. I used to sell high end business intelligence services to Fortune 500 companies. I was on the road all the time and it finally just got old. Early 2001 I abruptly left and started my own internet marketing company, but struggled *badly*.

When smart phones came out, I shifted to creating apps for businesses and was fairly successful with that, but I ended up with the problem of needing to travel all the time again. In 2011, I created my own app that really sort of flopped. I think I got maybe 5,000 total downloads. A month later, I created another app that got about double those numbers. A month later, another app that got even more still. I haven't looked back since.

Q: I see you found success through sheer tenacity. From what I understand, you outsource the entire programming and design aspect of all your apps. Have you had any difficulties in communicating exactly what you wanted to do while doing so?

A: I haven't had any problems, but then that's possibly because of my background, as I always have things pretty well documented. I give hand drawn wireframe diagrams of each screen, I describe every element of that screen, describe the purpose of it, and then I have a write up that describes the purpose and general functionality of the app.

Q: Do you think that you're at any sort of disadvantage without understanding the basics of iOS programming? How do

AppSource

you mitigate the risk that the programmers you hire might possibly take advantage of this situation?

A: That's a good question. Let me start by saying that I'm a techno-geek. I've been programming for a *very* long time (I wrote an operating system for a TRS 80 when I was sixteen), and I'm fairly familiar with iOS programming. So I'm going to answer this by telling you exactly what I tell other people in this scenario.

The first thing you need to do is get multiple quotes. This is especially important if it's the first app or even one of the first five apps that you're doing with any one programmer.

Even if you're just having a single screen added to an existing app, go out to oDesk or something and get multiple quotes. That will help you to know how much something should really cost and will prevent a programmer from trying to overcharge for something fairly simple.

One of the people on my list contacted me one time and said that their programmer wanted to charge them an extra $500 to add a "more" screen to their app, and I let them know it was a complete rip off. I then told them to go onto oDesk and post a job to do just that. He promptly got three programmers offering to do it for just $50 with the understanding that a good job would mean more work on other apps. The person he ended up choosing now does most of the apps for that guy, because the programmer doesn't try and rip him off like the first programmer tried to do.

Q: You mention starting 3 successful mobile app businesses that brought in $1.6 million in revenue in only 9 months. That's pretty impressive considering how most developers

seem to flounder in the App Store. Why do you think your apps became so successful, and what do you think you did right with that them?

A: Let me start by saying that going from zero to $1.6 million in 9 months will probably *not* happen for most people. I was able to do it because I understand how to *fully* monetize my apps.

As an example, most of that $1.6 million in revenue came from offering an extremely high-end coaching program that cost upwards of $50 grand just to get started.

Q: So the main purpose of the app was just to generate leads? Can you tell us more about these apps that you've developed?

A: Yup. Unfortunately, I can't tell you more about my apps at the moment. I create apps in niches that most people don't even think about and are largely ignored. I purposely 'fly under the radar' because I really would prefer people not to figure out exactly what I'm doing.

My apps are created under a fairly large list of separate developer accounts to prevent the true size and scope of what I'm doing becoming known. Basically, I don't want people 'following me around' in the app space. Sorry, I hope you understand.

Q: That's fine. Maybe you can tell us what you would do differently if you were starting out in iPhone app development all over again?

A: I wouldn't create any general or gaming apps at all and either go straight to creating apps for niches or simply create newsstand

AppSource

apps. In my opinion, the iTunes newsstand is currently the single most overlooked opportunity there is.

There are currently more than 900,000 apps in the App Store but as of right now, there're barely over 2,000 newsstand apps in total. It's a little easier to stand out from the crowd when you only have to compete against 2,000 apps instead of trying to compete in other crowded segments.

Aside from this, there are entire *categories* of possible markets to place a magazine that currently have nothing. The newsstand is the place to be looking at right now. In fact, I even created a special report called the Magazine Magnate that you can get when you purchase my *Appreneur* magazine app on iTunes. Currently it's only available on the iPad.

There're two special reports that you get for free, and you can get the first issue of the app on a 30-day free trial. In the first issue you can request the Magazine Magnate special report and get it for free as well.

Q: **Well, I guess that's one app you've developed that you're telling us about right there. Do you think there's a formula for success in the App Store? If so, what do you think that formula is?**

A: There are two main factors to success in the App Store, no question about it. They are:

1) Marketing your app

2) Monetizing your app

Without marketing, you can really sort of forget it. There're too many apps being published now. You have to get your app out there, people have to know about it and want it. Secondly, you have to know how you're going to make money from those apps.

Far too many people think they'll make money from iAds or something. The truth is that with the possible exception of RevMob, most of the advertising networks just won't make you very much even if you have millions of downloads. I go into more detailed ways of monetizing your apps in the first issue of *Appreneur*, which again is a free magazine app for iPad that you can get from iTunes.

Q: What were your biggest challenges and lessons learnt from releasing your first app? Would you create the same app today in a different way?

A: The single most important thing that I learned is that it's really all about the 'app network', a phrase I believe was first coined by Trey Smith. The App Network is when you have multiple apps that you can use in-app messaging and client-server integration with your nag screens to cross-promote your other apps to.

If you go into partnerships with other app developers and you all then cross-promote for each other (creating a 'network of networks'), then everyone can obtain even greater success.

Q: What's your process for going from app idea to full-blown development?

A: Document, document, document. Don't make your developers wonder what you might mean. Be short, concise, but make

AppSource

sure you explain as much as possible. Then, as soon as you can possibly afford it, hire a project manager that lives in the same city as your developers. A good, certified by the PMP, project manager is seriously worth their weight in gold. My project manager easily saves/makes me millions per year but his cost is only 80k. It's money very well spent.

Q: That's a thought echoed by Mike Milo and Chad Mureta as well. Do you conduct beta-tests with potential users for your apps? If so, how do you go about it?

A: I'm going to admit that my beta-testing process is fairly weak. I simply test out the apps myself on my own devices, running through each piece of functionality myself. That's really all I do. However, I also know that my project manager is testing the apps as well. Having said that, most of my apps are pretty darn simple and are built off of a custom template that makes bugs and the like far less likely.

Q: Now that there are more than 900,000 apps on the App Store, do you think that the market is becoming too saturated for the average independent developer to succeed?

A: Absolutely not. The truth is that the overwhelming majority of apps in the app store are poorly marketed (if they're marketed at all), and even more poorly monetized. While it's not quite as easy as it was a year ago, an app with decent marketing and good monetization can still make a killing with surprisingly little effort.

Q: So how do you think independent iPhone developers can succeed going forward?

A: The first thing to understand is that you probably will *not* hit a home run with your first app...or even your first 12! Keep creating apps, keep building your app network, and keep marketing your apps.

As you develop your experience, and especially if you follow the things I talk about in my App Developers Toolbox (again, free when you go to my website), you will build a steadily larger and larger app network which will make each subsequent app more successful. Additionally, joining other 'networks of networks' can *dramatically* help as well. While joining most of them (mine included) does come with some form of up front cost to make sure we're dealing with someone serious, the benefit *far* outweighs the cost. Then there's also setting up joint ventures with other app developers. Finally, there's also making sure that your apps are as completely monetized as possible.

Q: Why do you think most indie developers seem to have such a hard time making a living from selling their apps?

A: That's easy...little (or no) marketing and poor monetization. Like I said before, without these two factors, you might as well hang it up.

Q: What words of advice would you have for someone just starting out in iOS development?

A: Don't give up. Follow the advice I've mentioned previously, and understand that it will take creating more than a few apps before you can expect to see any significant money coming in.

AppSource

Q: What online resources would you recommend for app development?

A: Honestly, I don't use anything. I get daily updates from my developers, on top of the daily updates that I get from my project manager. In fact let me say now that anyone looking to get into app development would probably be well served to learn a little about project management and how to manage projects remotely. There are usually several books on this topic in any major bookstore. I personally can't recommend any because it's been probably 10 years since I last needed to look at a book on this topic.

Q: Do you develop for the iPad? What do you think are the advantages/disadvantages of focusing on the iPad?

A: I'm getting to the point that I'm starting to develop almost exclusively for iPad. The reason for this (and it's obvious that I'm doing this, my *Appreneur* Magazine is available only on iPad) is simple.

iPads are 'accessory devices'. That means that you don't *need* an iPad. You get one because you want one. Almost everything you can do on an iPad you can already do on your phone or computer. Furthermore, they are expensive.

The simple fact that someone is using your app on an iPad tells you two things. They have disposable income (or else they couldn't afford the iPad) and they have disposable time (or else they wouldn't be using your app).

This is the best possible 'lead' you can have. If your apps are free or somehow follow the Freemium model, then you don't have to worry about the person looking at your app being too broke to afford a few in-app upgrades.

Q: What's currently your favorite iOS app, and why?

A: I'm going to have to give you two, because I use them together. *Draw* for iPad and *Evernote*. The reason is that between those two apps, I can completely explain an entire app idea anywhere that I am, and then easily get that idea to my project manager to be placed into the development queue.

Q: What is your development setup like? How large is your development team?

A: I have a virtual assistant, a project manager and six developers that work for me full time.

Q: What marketing do you do for your apps and how do you go about doing it?

A: Of course! I definitely market my apps, and I don't *usually* spend any money doing so, though I have been playing around with some paid advertising here and there. Not too much though, until I can get better testing numbers.

As for how...that's a tough question because it depends on the app. I'll participate in forums well ahead of the app going live, then when it does, tell the forum about it. I'll find blogs and websites in the target market and give them the app for free in

AppSource

exchange for a review (and I ask that the review be honest, they don't have to blow smoke).

There are a few other things that I do, but the overwhelming majority of my time and effort is focused on these two things. Just keep in mind that this works because I don't do games. I create niche apps for niche markets.

Q: You mention playing around with paid advertising. What's that been like so far?

A: Well, as I said, I haven't done very much yet. Thus far the ROI hasn't really been all that great, not much better than break even. However I also haven't put much effort into it either so I can't give you a definitive answer.

Q: In your website, you mention using your knowledge of web marketing (traffic generation and conversion) to grow your app companies. Care to elaborate on that?

A: Hopefully I don't come off sounding like a jerk but I already did! Basically it's the forum marketing and talking to owners of other websites to promote my apps for me. There're a small number of SEO-related things that I do, but again, the forums and the other websites/ blogs are where the majority of my downloads come from.

Q: It's also been mentioned that a 'Launch Strategy' is becoming increasingly important towards getting eyeballs for apps, with bigger developers paying high amounts per user for the indirect benefit of being seen on the charts.

What are your thoughts on this? Do you think it's an ethical practice?

A: First, let me say that it's completely ethical. In fact, if you're smart you will also have some kind of a launch for your apps. Now if you don't have a huge budget, there are ways of getting around that by paying commissions based on sales. This way the people that help to promote your launch get paid based on the benefit they bring to you, and you don't have to pay anything out until you've actually got money in hand.

Q: The buzzword for a while now in the app developer scene is Freemium. Do you think that pursuing this strategy will continue to be feasible over the long haul? What are your thoughts on how app monetization will change in the future?

A: In my opinion the Freemium model ... or even 'Premium Plus' as I like to call it (a paid app that *also* has in-app purchases available) is the ONLY way to go.

Take the *Appreneur* app as an example. The app itself is free, and when you get it, you can get two special reports right out of the gate without paying for anything. Then you can get a 30 day free trial which will give you the first issue (where I cover more app marketing and monetization than is in the app toolbox) without having to pay anything.

However, as I and my partners roll forward in that effort (http://appclover.com), we'll have other larger reports and information products that you'll have to pay for, on top of the monthly membership that we'll be getting.

AppSource

But look at it like this, the monthly magazine subscription will allow us to give more and better information than we could POSSIBLY give on an on-going basis if it was just free or just a single 99 cent purchase.

Getting just $0.99 for a download really won't cut it unless you can get millions of downloads. Somewhere I read that the hugely popular Temple Run game was at one time a $0.99 game. When they made it free, and added in the in-app purchases, the game became much more successful and is making them much more money.

Q: Great. We've come to the end of the interview and this sure turned out to be a really insightful session. Thanks again for taking the time out to do this!

A: Sure thing. You're welcome.

Chapter 8
Isabelle Thomas Duston

◆

The MBA Who Started An App Development Company

With exorbitant student fees, outstanding loans to pay and a multitude of companies looking to hire you (well, at least in the past!), most MBA's usually seek out high-paying jobs in the finance and consulting industries by the time they graduate. Only a select few move into entrepreneurship, and out of these few, lesser still move into the world of app development.

Isabelle Thomas Duston, a French native residing in the US, is one of these rare few. A graduate from ESCP Europe, one of the best business schools in Europe, she set up Apps of All Nations LLC after leaving her husband at the peak of the recession and realizing she needed to be financially independent to support her two young children.

With no option but to succeed, she acted quickly when she realized that the majority of apps were only available in English, putting together a team to develop *iCooking*, a cooking app available in multiple languages. *iCooking* then went on to become a major hit on the App Store, garnering nearly half a million downloads to date.

***

AppSource

Q: Hi Isabelle. Could you please tell us a little about your background and how you got into iPhone app development?

A: I am a French businesswoman and entrepreneur living in the U.S. with my three children. I have an MBA from ESCP-Europe, ranked the number one best business school in Europe in 2010. As a serial entrepreneur, I have a firm belief in the use of mobile technology to stimulate educational growth and social change.

My first app endeavor, Apps of All Nations, LCC, began when I noticed a gap in a niche market. When the iPhone first came out, the majority of apps were only available in English. Acting quickly, I used my determination, creativity and love for language – I speak five – and put a team together that created *iCooking* – a cooking app available in multiple languages.

Q: That's an interesting background. I think you're the first developer I've spoken to that has an MBA. From what I understand, you outsource the entire programming and design aspect of all your apps. Have you had any difficulties in communicating exactly what you wanted to do while doing so?

A: I've been fortunate not to have too many problems. Actually, when I wrote my first specification, the developer I used told me that my specification was very precise. I also hired a project manager who works for Curriki, and has been writing specification for years. It probably helps that I avoid subcontracting outside the US.

Q: Can you tell us a little more about the type of apps that you're focusing on right now?

Chapter: 8

A: I'm passionate about education and utilizing the potential of digital media to engage children in the learning process.

I am committed to providing innovative solutions in the fields of education and literacy. Our latest app, *Smart4Kids* will offer an educational app in English before eventually being released in other languages. *Smart4Kids* was developed by educators and offers 36 lessons to support budding readers. We plan to launch the product in September.

Q: Do you think that you're at any sort of disadvantage without understanding the basics of iOS programming? How do you mitigate the risk that the programmers you hire might possibly take advantage of this situation?

A: Yes there is a risk. However I hired developers from small companies, who were trying to do the best work they could in as little time as possible. They made a quote according a very precise specification. It was not in their interest to try to take advantage of me, especially if they wanted repeat business. Moreover, once you have developed a few apps, you know roughly how much time it should take.

Q: How has *iCooking* done to date in the App Store? How have sales/downloads been like?

A: We've had 491,900 paid and free downloads so far with sales tallying around $260,000.

Q: That's very impressive. Did you expect *iCooking* to be as successful as it was? Why do you think it became so successful, and what do you think you did right with that it?

A: *iCooking* began with fifteen cookbooks available in French and English, and grew from there to over one hundred and eighty books in over ten languages. Again, I think it was a matter of finding a gap in the market and acting quickly. Finding the right people is always part of that, and I have been very blessed to put together a great team at the right time.

The main reason for its success is the fact that the apps are in the customer's native language. It's also a simple app that can be used without a Wi-Fi connection.

However, Apple doesn't seem to agree that people need apps in their language, and they have recently rejected all my new apps, arguing that everyone speaks English, therefore having cookbooks in Portuguese, Polish or Swedish would not meet any customer expectation.

Q: That doesn't really make much sense but unfortunately, you've got to play by Apple's logic if you want to be in the App Store. You mentioned not having similar success with your second project, *iStory*. Why do you think the concept didn't take off as planned?

A: The *iStory* project was only for the iPad, therefore the number of potential owners is much lower. The apps are for four to six year old children and iPad owners possibly do not feel comfortable letting their young children play with such expensive devices.

The competition is very important; everybody thinks that making interactive children books for the iPad is a very cool idea. My own developer created a company that would do only that and it was a total failure. It seems that the people who buy, tend to choose the books they liked when they were kids, like Dr. Seuss.

Q: I'm not so sure if it's the case that iPad owners are uncomfortable with letting their young children use the iPad though. Children's education and games seem to be thriving industries on the iPad at the moment, and the iPad seems to be a perfect fit as an electronic babysitter to pacify children while the parents do something else.

If you were starting out again in iPhone app development though, what would you do differently?

A: From a development standpoint, I think using a subcontractor is fine.

From a marketing standpoint, I would be very careful. Very few people make money selling apps; you really need a portfolio. Moreover, most ideas already exist. Getting noticed on the store is almost impossible nowadays. Personally, I think it only makes sense as a tool to improve a business you already have.

Q: That's a pretty strong statement. It's definitely a lot harder than it used to be but I'd say there're still gaps of opportunity. It's just probably a lot harder to find! What do you think is the formula for success on the App Store now then?

A: I hate to say it but there's a lot of luck involved. It's all about the Apple team noticing you and putting you forward.

Aside from that, you have to answer a real need, make sure what you have in mind does not already exist, and that people will benefit from the app. Make sure your costs are as low as possible, and be ready to fail before you eventually succeed.

AppSource

Q: Can you tell us about some of the challenges you faced in releasing *iCooking*?

A: You may find your app perfect, but not everybody will. The first few negative 1 star reviews are hard to take. It can be very frustrating not to be able to answer your unsatisfied customers, who are generally the ones leaving comments. Just be ready to accept this and move on.

Q: That's definitely frustrating. It's unfortunate that Apple doesn't have a mechanism to allow developers to respond to reviews. Matthew Panzarino of *The Next Web* recently discussed how the ability to respond to reviews on the App Store is the most wanted feature by iOS developers.

Can you tell us about your process for going from app idea to full-blown development?

A: Sure. First I design a mock-up of the flow. I then discuss it with my team to try and see what I have missed out, and whether we have a flow that is as simple as it can be. Then I get my graphic designer to create mock-ups of various screens, and these mock-ups once again go through a process of validation with the team.

The project manager writes the specification, the graphic designer creates each of the necessary elements, then the developer starts working. We try to get a build every day, and we test and debug along the way.

Q: How do you think independent iPhone developers can succeed going forward?

A: If the independent iPhone developer works for people who need to get apps done and is paid for the development, then yes, he/she can be successful. The time when developers can sell their own apps and live on that income is over.

Q: That's another strong statement coming from you! I don't necessarily agree with you on that but I can see where you're coming from. Things have certainly changed a lot for iPhone app developers over the past few years. Given that you're not particularly bullish on the industry, what words of advice would you have for someone just starting out in iOS development?

A: Collaboration is the key; work with great designers, developers and people who are proficient and passionate about the field you intend to develop apps for. They need to have current access to the market.

Q: What do you think are the pros and cons of focusing on the iPad?

A: I made that mistake. I would not do it again–an app that only exists on the iPad has very little chance to be sustainable.

Q: I wouldn't go that far but it definitely is a smaller market. I've met a number of developers who focus specifically on the iPad and seem to be doing OK though. What's currently your favorite iOS app, and why?

A: My favorite apps tend to be apps which make my life easier–Banking apps and *Dropbox* come to mind.

My kids buy way more apps than I do!

AppSource

Q: Can you tell us what your development setup is like? How large is your development team?

A: I have one full time programmer, and several contract graphic designers.

Q: Do you do any marketing for your apps, and if so how do you go about doing it?

A: Marketing is very expensive and has never worked for me. I intend to do some marketing for my reading app, but I think it'll be easier to connect with my target audience via a blog that focuses on children and education.

Q: Well, that's one form of marketing right there. So I take it you haven't experienced much success with paid advertising?

A: Nope. Online advertising with Google ads and Facebook ads didn't work out well for us at all.

Q: It's also been mentioned that a 'Launch Strategy' is becoming increasingly important towards getting eyeballs for apps, with bigger developers paying high amounts per user for the indirect benefit of being seen on the charts.

What are your thoughts on this?

A: I have tried something similar, but it is *very* expensive and seems to have a short-term effect. There is no magic formula to stay on top of the charts. Your apps has to answer a need (I am not talking about games), and be *really* good.

Q: The buzzword for a while now in the app developer scene is Freemium. Do you think that pursuing this strategy will continue to be feasible over the long haul?

A: I personally would be reluctant to go Freemium, especially in the field of education. What's a good strategy for games might not make as much sense for the other categories.

Q: OK great. It's been a good chat. Thanks for the interview!

A: Thanks for having me.

Chapter 9
Michael Jacobs

◆

Simplifying The Process Of Networking With *SociaLink*

Picking himself up after two failed tech ventures, Michael Jacobs was determined to push on, coming up with the idea for *SociaLink*, a mobile application that simplifies the way people network, while on a study abroad program in India.

After interviewing multiple development companies while he was in Bangalore, Michael eventually decided on a team and managed the project from the US after he returned home.

Aside from being a mobile app fanatic and creator of *SociaLink*, he is also the author of an ebook on app development, *Making Your Idea An App Store App – 8 Secrets Behind Creating A Successful Mobile App*. All this and he's only twenty-one years old!

After a slow start, *SociaLink* is picking up traction and has since been featured in the June 2013 issue of Entrepreneur Magazine.

***

Q: Hi Michael. Could you please tell us a little about your background and how you got into iPhone app development?

A: Sure thing. I kind of got into the technology realm as a freshman in college, where I started a company based on a new website concept where college students could share their experiences and all the content would be user-generated.

While the startup didn't take off as I expected, I did gain valuable experience from running it. This past summer, while I was traveling in India, I came up with a mobile app idea that I couldn't stop thinking about. I started talking to development companies in Bangalore about building the app and eventually found one I liked enough to hire. It all really just started from having that idea I couldn't stop thinking about, and then just making things happen.

Q: That's pretty nifty. Probably helped that you were right smack in Outsource Central as well. Do you outsource the entire programming and design aspect of all your apps? Have you had any difficulties in communicating exactly what you wanted to do while doing so?

A: Yes, I do. I originally thought of collaborating with some friends who were coders to build the app but eventually thought better of the idea. I wanted to develop something polished so that I could compete properly in the App Store.

And yes, there are definitely difficulties in communication but my experience hasn't been as bad as some of the stories I've heard from other developers. Sometimes, there's a little confusion regarding what I wanted but the difficulties have been minor so far. It's honestly not bad at all in my experience. We work fairly well together, and if there are issues that need to be settled, we just get on Skype and hash things out. There were a couple of late nights involved when things had to really be spelt out clearly but it was still a good experience overall.

Q: Roughly how long did the development of SociaLink take by outsourcing it this way?

A: I'd say the entire process was around four to five months.

Q: Great. Did you sign an NDA with your developers and do you think this is necessary?

A: With my developers, I actually signed a contract with them but at the start, when I first approached them with the idea, we did sign an NDA as well. It's debatable how necessary the NDA is. Personally, I think it's important to do so, especially with the development team that you eventually settle with. It's also not much extra effort to get one done just for legal purposes.

However, I've noticed other entrepreneurs going around asking people to sign NDAs when they're 'sharing' the idea. That doesn't really make any sense to me. I personally love sharing my ideas with other people because that's how I get different perspectives on what I'm doing, and it all blends together into helping me build the best product possible.

Q: I understand that you don't come from a programming background. Do you think that you're at any sort of disadvantage without understanding the basics of iOS programming?

A: Oh definitely, that's why I'm starting to teach myself how to code right now! I recently had a conversation with a good friend who's a pretty high-level programmer, and we were discussing our visions of what the future of the industry would be like.

I thought it was really interesting how he managed to detail his vision based on how the development process was changing. I think a fundamental understanding of the basics of iOS programming will probably make me a better entrepreneur in the long run.

Q: How do you mitigate the risk that the programmers you hire might possibly take advantage of this situation?

A: This was actually a major concern of mine regarding all the development teams I looked at. I'd heard all the horror stories about outsourcing to India and ending up with completely no product and losing all your money.

What I personally did to try and circumvent this was to do a boatload of research. I researched all the different companies I was looking at. I looked at all the reviews they had, downloaded and used all the different apps they had created, and spoke to as many of their previous clients as I could find. This was how I got a feel of which company would be the most professional and fit in nicely with my situation.

Q: Considering that you used a development company, what do you think are the advantages and disadvantages of going with a development company as opposed to using an independent contractor?

A: I don't really see too many disadvantages to using a reputable development company. Maybe the service won't be as personalized but that's not really a big deal for me.

I think one of the biggest advantages of using a development company was that I never had to worry too much about response

AppSource

time. If one person on the team wasn't available for whatever reason, there would always be another person to help out. This constant ease of contact made for very smooth communication and I never really had to worry about knocking on my contractor's door for not answering my calls!

Q: If you were starting out again in iPhone app development, what would you do differently?

A: To be honest with you, I'd have done a lot more research on the marketing front. When I was developing the app, there were quite a number of times when I'd be working on the app with my developers from around 8pm to 3am as those would be the working hours in India's time zone.

I just wish I'd spent most of those days focusing on marketing instead and getting better prepared for app launch. For example, doing things such as building a pre-launch list and optimizing a Facebook and Twitter page for launch. Oh well, there's always next time.

Q: Do you think there's a formula for success in the App Store, and if so, what do you think that formula is?

A: I don't think there's necessarily a formula because there're just so many different ways in which you can find success on the App Store. However, I do think there are a couple of ways you can increase your chances:

1. Have a unique idea. It doesn't have to be an idea that nobody has ever seen before, but it has to be something that stands out from the clutter in the App Store. This way, you increase the odds of having your app go viral.

2. Take an existing app that's already out there and improve it. There are so many things you can do. You can add additional features, make it more user-friendly, or come up with a better design.

Q: It's probably not going to be so easy to come up with a unique idea now that there are more than 900,000 apps on the App Store! Do you think that the market is becoming too saturated for the average independent developer to succeed?

A: Definitely. It's getting harder and harder by the day. However I think at the same time, as the App Store continues to grow, there'll be additional ways and means of marketing apps that'll make it easier for developers to get their apps in front of people, and it'll be up to the developers to experiment with these new methods.

For the most part, the landscape is probably going to be tougher for indie developers. While it's definitely harder to come up with something original that the App Store hasn't already seen, if you *can* come up with one, that's going to be key in rising above the noise.

Q: What were your biggest challenges and lessons learnt from releasing *SociaLink*?

A: I think anytime you release a product, no matter how many times you do it, you'll face challenges! Frankly, the biggest challenge for me was taking that first step into making *SociaLink* an actual product, as opposed to just an idea... to actually go out there and get a product launched. It was taking that first step and finally taking action to make my idea a reality.

AppSource

I actually think this is the biggest challenge for so many people who want to be entrepreneurs, but just end up spending most of their time just talking about ideas and 'strategies'. It was exactly the same case for me as well. I was always talking about different app ideas but I just could never take that first step towards executing that idea.

Q: Well, thankfully you've already cleared that hurdle with the release of *SociaLink*. Do you conduct beta-tests with potential users for your apps? If you do, how do you go about it?

A: Yup, I had about ten to twenty potential users, all of whom were friends and family. We let them play around with the app, paid attention to whether they could intuitively grasp how to use it, and took note of any difficulties they had using it.

We would go back and forth with our beta-testers this way, refining the app each time and making adjustments as required.

Q: How do you think independent iPhone app developers can succeed going forward?

A: I would say to just think differently and not to blindly follow current trends. For example, every other developer seemed to be making map apps because of all that fuss over how Apple's map app didn't make the cut. It'd be great if you were one of the first few on the scene but now that's been done to death already.

Also, keep moving forward. Even when things aren't working out the way you want them to, keep pushing on. If your launch doesn't work out so well, focus on figuring out why, and learn new ways to market the app *after* the launch. Don't give up. Even

Chapter: 9

if your app doesn't become a success, you'll have gained that much more knowledge to help make your next one a hit.

Q: Why do you think most indie developers seem to have such a hard time making a living from selling their own apps?

A: I think one of the reasons could be because of the way users search for apps on the App Store. Personally, and this goes for a number of people I know as well, I don't go onto the App Store to just randomly browse apps.

I'm guessing that most users go on the App Store to look for certain utility apps that they need or to look for a specific app that their friends told them about. This makes it very difficult for an indie developer to get noticed unless they receive a feature from Apple or they've cracked the top charts for their category.

It's very difficult to get an app to go viral. I can't tell you how many review sites I'd gotten to review my apps that didn't net me more than twenty to twenty-five downloads.

Q: Do you do any marketing for your apps, and if so how do you go about doing it?

A: Yeah, definitely. I've run a bunch of social media campaigns–Facebook, Twitter, the usual stuff. I spend a lot of time on video marketing, creating unique videos for *SociaLink* and trying to get the videos to go viral.

We're also currently working on our blog and we're going to be launching it soon. We're quite reliant on word of mouth. What has gotten us the most downloads so far is networking, meeting

AppSource

new people and getting them to try our app. Usually, if they like the app, they'll share it with their friends and we end up with more downloads.

We've also been focusing on getting bloggers to write about the app and getting other forms of press. A big success for us on this front has been getting a feature in Entrepreneur magazine.

We have some new marketing campaigns that we're going to explore but nothing's set in stone yet, so we don't really have too much else to say about that!

Q: Congrats on the feature in Entrepreneur magazine! Have you done any paid advertising, and if so, have you seen any Return on Investment (ROI) on it?

A: Not yet. We've been concentrating on free resources right now but we're thinking about trying out paid advertising – most probably Facebook ads. Currently, we're doing the research into whether paying for ads will be worthwhile.

Q: What online resources do you use and recommend for app development?

A: Currently, we're mainly using Testflight. We use it for distributing the app to our beta-testers for feedback. Aside from that, we don't really use anything else.

Q: It's also been mentioned that a 'Launch Strategy' is becoming increasingly important towards getting eyeballs for apps, with bigger developers paying high amounts per user for the indirect benefit of being seen on the charts.

Chapter: 9

What are your thoughts on this? Do you think it's an ethical practice?

A: Well, it's definitely annoying for smaller developers like us. I don't really think the issue is so much whether it's ethical or unethical, but just how much you're willing to pay to acquire a customer.

These guys have the marketing budget to be able to do this, so us indies have to find different ways of competing. If I had the money, I'd probably be doing the same myself.

Q: Ok, we'll wrap things up now. Thanks for the interview!

A: Thanks for having me.

Chapter 10
Mike Milo

◆

Outsourcing A Cash-Positive App Business That Helps Change The Lives Of Children Around The World

I first came across Mike's story when I was reading Pat Flynn's excellent blog, Smart Passive Income. It was an interesting blog post on how Mike was changing lives and making a healthy living by developing speech therapy iPhone apps for children.

I was intrigued by his story, but I was even more intrigued by the fact that he was earning about ten to twenty thousand dollars a month outsourcing his *entire* operations. This was after hiring engineers, designers and a project manager to look after all aspects of development! It was an amazing feat and while the interview was very thorough, I was curious to find out more about how he managed his business.

Here was someone with no relevant experience who'd managed to enter a hungry niche that didn't have many people serving it. Together with his wife Poorani, Mike realized that there was a dearth of speech therapy tools for children, and that the iOS platform would be the perfect medium for such tools. Sensing a great business opportunity on the horizon, both of them decided to pursue the idea of developing apps for speech therapy.

Today, they run a cash-positive business that helps change the lives of children and parents around the world.

***

Q: Hi Mike. Could you please tell us a little about your background and how you got into iPhone app development?

A: Sure. My wife, Poorani, is a Speech-Language Pathologist and she's the brains of our operation. She started using the iPad in therapy and loved it.

She told me that there was a real dearth of apps for her kids (this was about 2 years ago). I am not an engineer, but I am a tech enthusiast who's always looking out for interesting business opportunities. Once we started talking about it, I knew that we could create something good for kids.

At worst, I figured it would be a very expensive tool that my wife could use in therapy–there are plenty of those! So we built the app and it did fairly well. This gave us the confidence to start churning out more and more apps.

My background is in product management and marketing for web-based tools. With my wife's creative talent and my practical knowledge, we make a good team!

Q: From what I understand, you outsource the entire programming and design aspect of all your apps. Have you encountered any difficulties in communicating exactly what you wanted while doing so?

AppSource

A: Absolutely. Whether your products are made in your living room or overseas, communication is always the biggest challenge. I kicked off our first app as a tyrant, trying to control every aspect of design and development.

I realized fairly quickly that my engineers and designer were much better at this than me. It is one thing to be on a project and manage with an iron fist to ensure that no mistakes are made. However, because I was trying to build a company, I focused on building trust and familiarity with everyone.

Even with trust, things can still go awry, so I require an update every day in order to know what has been worked on and if they are off track. I also get frequent builds and use a detailed issue list to manage each issue.

Q: Is there any disadvantage in not understanding the basics of iOS programming? How do you mitigate the risk that the programmers you hire might possibly take advantage of this situation?

A: I honestly don't think so. I think it probably liberates me a bit from some of the details, so I can focus on other things like marketing and strategy. I am sure I do miss some details that an engineer would not, but it allows me to look at it from a user's standpoint.

I mitigate the risk by testing early and often. I also try to get an understanding of how long it takes to complete a task, so I can keep track. Again, a lot of it comes down to trust, and I trust both our engineers and designer.

Chapter: 10

Q: How have your apps done to date in the App Store since you started developing apps?

A: So far we've been doing quite well. We have over 100,000 downloads, and continue to grow.

Q: Those are awesome numbers. Did you expect your apps to be as successful as they were? Why do you think they became so successful, and what do you think you did right with that them?

A: I was pretty sure that we would be successful but our apps have certainly exceeded expectations. At the risk of sounding like a jerk, I think they were successful because they are good products.

Each app is designed to tackle a small but important aspect of Speech Therapy. Instead of trying to build something broad, we focused and built each app to do only one thing very well. We put a lot of thought into the character and brand so the success would be long-term, and not just one good app with no follow up. I would say that building the brand and the character was the smartest thing that we did since we are now probably one of the best known brands in our niche.

Q: With your success in the App Store, it seems that your focus is on speech therapy, and you've definitely carved out a nice niche for yourself in that category. Do you have any thoughts on expanding to other categories though?

A: It sure is tempting. I would like nothing better than to build a fantasy baseball app or one of the many other apps that I would love to have. But I think my wife has a better head than my own for

AppSource

brainstorming great apps. We have barely scratched the surface with technological solutions in her field. We have to focus if we are going to continue to innovate.

Q: That makes sense, especially since you've found a niche that is receptive to what you're offering. I think these are the pockets of opportunity for developers to break into the market, and it'll be reserved for those who can identify these niches and cater to them. The ones best primed for success will be those who understand the pain points of these niches and can build apps to serve them–like you guys!

If you were starting out in iPhone app development again, what would you do differently?

A: I'd do a lot of things different. The biggest one is to forge partnerships and networks. I was so paranoid that our ideas would get stolen that I was reluctant to meet with like-minded people. I learned a ton and was super inspired once I started going to Meetups on children's apps or education.

I wish I had done this earlier. It would have saved me a lot of trouble and mistakes if I had spoken to somebody that had done it before.

Q: Wow, I'm impressed that there's a Meetup group for children's apps. Seems like there're Meetup groups for almost everything nowadays!

You mentioned wishing you had done this earlier as it would have saved you a lot of trouble and mistakes. Can you give us examples of what you picked up from these Meetup sessions?

Chapter: 10

A: It's tough to come up with specifics since I've picked up so many things. Most of my examples are pretty boring though. They're usually detail-oriented stuff such as, "The blue button on your homepage didn't catch my attention." These things are very important though.

Like any other profession, it is critical to speak to your colleagues to identify problems or opportunities. Many of them have feedback on what is going on in the industry. They know many of your clients just as well as you do, but may have a completely different perspective. I have also come across great opportunities during these Meetups. For example, we have been able to speak at Apple twice now, and this would never have happened if we hadn't gotten close to some great people in our industry (in this case Moms with Apps and Go Go Mongo).

Q: Do you think there's a formula for success in the App Store? If so, what do you think that formula is?

A: I think the closest thing to a successful formula is to make sure that you build something either better or cheaper than the next guy. There will always be competition. The only way to compete is to do it better or cheaper- preferably both.

That said, there are a lot of very good apps out there that don't do well. Getting discovered is quite a challenge, especially with the number of apps out there now.

Q: It's also getting harder to go cheaper as well. The majority of apps seem to be priced at $0.99 to $1.99, if they aren't going free!

What were your biggest challenges and lessons learnt from releasing your first app? Would you create the same app today in a different way?

A: Boy, there were countless challenges along the way! The toughest was probably figuring out how to obtain all the assets needed to make the app–images, sounds, music, etc.

We got lucky on a couple of fronts. We have a good friend who is a musician who let us record in his studio. For the animations and artwork, we found an incredible talent. He was able to put together all the artwork with the guidance of our engineers. Everything was trial and error. The key for me was being dumb enough not to be discouraged by all the setbacks. As far as lessons learned, one of the key things is to always provide the content upfront (audio, graphics, etc.). I know it sounds simple, but I tend to get all excited and want to start right away. It leads to higher cost and a longer time to market if you put them to work, but then have downtime while you track down content or answer questions.

Regarding whether I would create the app in a different way- I don't think I'd do too many things differently. I really like the way it turned out.

Q: Do you have a process for going from app idea to full-blown development?

A: We have modified our process as our experience has grown. I was extremely thorough with our first app and gave our engineers as much as I could possibly document. I created storyboards, use cases, personas- all kinds of things. I think all of this was very helpful for our engineers since it was our first app. Now, we have a much deeper relationship with our engineers and designers. I can describe in a few pages what we need. Like I said before, have everything ready up front though.

Chapter: 10

One important thing is to bounce your idea off other people. Make sure that people would actually pay for it and want to use it. I tend to fall in love with an idea, and need a reality check sometimes. Find somebody who will be honest with you and say, "No, that's a bad idea".

Q: Do you conduct beta-tests with potential users for your apps? If you do, how do you go about it?

A: We are lucky because we have built in beta-testers from my wife's practice. She works with the exact kids whom we want to buy our apps. She typically knows what apps to build because she has a real need in therapy. We just build what she needs.

Q: That's extremely fortunate. Most app developers don't have a ready, in-built target audience to use their apps. Now that there are about 900,000 apps on the App Store, do you think that the market is becoming too saturated for the average independent developer to succeed?

A: I don't think so but it's certainly not going to get easier! We live in an amazing time where it is actually possible for a guy in his living room to build a better app than a million dollar company. I think the thing that we little guys have going for us is that we are nimble and willing to take risks.

Bigger companies are hesitant to take the risks that may be required to make a good app. Also, their production costs are much higher, so much so that their ROI wouldn't be great if they expanded into niche categories.

I think the games category is probably where they hold a substantial edge. Some of the game apps out are absolutely amazing. That's a tough market where you either make millions or absolutely nothing! I think the place for independents is in niche markets, where you can legitimately produce something better than an established company.

Q: How do you think independent iPhone developers can succeed going forward?

A: I think the key to success is in branding. Build something great and make your brand stand for something. In the Children's Education realm, the larger companies are starting to enter. People trust them since they have a long history of creating great products. The only way that I can compete with them is to counter with a great brand that people recognize.

Q: Why do you think most indie developers seem to have such a hard time making a living from selling their own apps?

A: It's hard to do. Starting your own business is tough in any industry–I don't think apps are much different. I am always surprised at how many people are able to make a living off an industry that they hadn't heard of just a few years ago.

I think many go into building an app with unrealistic expectations of instant profits. It takes just as much time and energy as starting up any other business to be successful.

Q: Yup, we can blame popular media for that! What words of advice do you have for someone just starting out in iPhone development?

A: Probably the same stuff that they've read and heard a hundred times before, but it holds true. Spend some time really vetting and mapping out your idea and asking tough questions.

What problem are you trying to solve?

How are you going to do it better than the competitors currently out there?

How are they going to find you?

Why would they tell their friends about your app?

If you think critically about all these questions, and you still feel like you have a viable idea that can make money, then do it. Surround yourself with good people, and figure out a way to do it.

Q: Aside from App Annie, which you mentioned on Pat Flynn's podcast, do you use any other online resources for app development?

A: I'm using Test Flight. Love it! It's a great service.

The two most important resources to me are:

(1) Google Docs- to track issues with the engineers

(2) Dropbox- to share content like images and audio.

AppSource

I recently discovered Google Hangout, which is a fantastic way to have a conversation as though you are in the same room with multiple people. The quality is better than Skype.

I also use Evernote as a place to store all my ideas.

Q: Do you develop for the iPad? What do you think are the advantages/disadvantages of focusing on the iPad?

A: Yes, all of our apps are universal. It is absolutely necessary for children's apps. For other apps, think about how you see people using the app.

It's not just the size of the screen- the two forms are completely different. The iPhone is on the go and a utility, but it is also a great time waster for games and news. The iPad is more of a device that you lounge around and use. Many people jump in without thinking about how the app will be used by the consumer, so you've got to really think it through.

Q: What's currently your favorite iOS app, and why?

A: I'll give you two answers–a business one and a fun one.

My favorite business app is *Quick Password Manager* (by 14773 Stones). You will see that when you start developing an app, you end up with alot of logins! You'll have iTunes, Paypal, Wordpress, etc. Also, my memory is shot! I spent way too much energy trying to stay consistent or remembering old ones. This app simply stores your passwords. I use it about twice a day.

Chapter: 10

The app I play for leisure is *Osmos HD* for iPad (by Hemisphere Games). It's a ridiculously beautiful game, super addictive and a brilliant concept.

Q: I'm personally using *1Password*. These password management tools are an absolute lifesaver in terms of keeping track of all your logins.

What is your development setup like? How large is your development team?

A: We have one dedicated Project Manager. Our engineering team varies depending on our needs. All of my communication is directly with our PM. Our designer is separate from the development team. My engineering team is fantastic, but their focus has not traditionally been with design. So I went out and found a great designer.

Q: **What is the exact nature of your project manager's role? Is there a reason why you don't fulfill this function yourself?**

A: If you are offshoring your work, you absolutely need a project manager. I am guessing that everybody has a project manager. They probably just don't know it (or they have a lead developer that fills the role).

This doesn't mean that I am off the hook for managing the project. I still have to be very involved and give the direction. I feel that the best work is done when you allow your developers to act independently. However, they need to be very buttoned up in order to act independently. This requires a lead that knows the big picture and all the important milestones. They can figure out the tactical approach so long as they meet all my requirements.

Q: That's an interesting take on things. Let's move along to the marketing segment of the interview now. How do you go about marketing your apps? Do you have a marketing budget?

A: Most of my marketing is simply reaching out to reviewers and users of our apps directly or trying to build up our Facebook/Twitter profiles. This is mainly for cost reasons. We do some advertising with sites that we feel are in line with the values of our users. We also offer other promotional materials with stickers and bumper magnets. Recently, we began selling Milo stuffed animals. This should prove to be a good way to market our business in a unique way. We want to be more than just an app company, and this is a step towards this.

Our marketing budget has been pretty meager since we are putting most of our money into development. We will be much more active this year starting with our new app, *Back to School*.

Q: I think selling Milo stuffed animals is a great way of branding your business, and could turn out to be a decent income stream. Angry Birds plush toy sales have already doubled to $400 million last year!

Did you do any paid advertising, and if so, have you seen any Return on Investment (ROI) on it?

A: I've done a little bit, but nothing substantial. At this point, I am trying to expand awareness, so it is not all about ROI. We will be more diligent with ROI in next year's cycle.

Chapter: 10

Q: How important do you think constant updates are for a successful app?

A: Updates are tricky because you lose those precious ratings when you deliver an update (or rather they are buried under the previous version). Because of this negative effect, we are very careful to only update when we are fixing a bug or adding a must-have feature. We are a little different from most other developers because our apps are fairly straightforward and don't require many updates.

Q: It's also been mentioned that a 'Launch Strategy' is becoming increasingly important towards getting eyeballs for apps, with bigger developers paying high amounts per user for the indirect benefit of being seen on the charts.

What are your thoughts on this? Do you think it's an ethical practice?

A: I have no problem with them paying more in advertising to get users. That's just the way it goes. Apple has cracked down on the more unethical marketing businesses lately, so the market is fair as far as I am concerned.

It is not necessarily a level playing field–most small setups have less resources and money than the larger developers. We just have to outwork them.

Q: The buzzword for a while now in the app developer scene is Freemium. Do you think that pursuing this strategy will continue to be feasible over the long haul? What are your thoughts on how app monetization will change in the future?

AppSource

A: Freemium has been very successful for a lot of people. I think it's possibly getting a little annoying for consumers and that can lead to some bad feelings (and bad ratings). I have always preferred the straightforward model of charging upfront mainly because we are marketing towards parents and teachers.

It just seems like a better model. I do think that Freemium has its place, and will continue to be around. It is a good way to make more money in the long run, you just have to be very good at getting a high conversion rate without upsetting people.

One shortcoming of our pay-up-front and in-app-purchase (IAP) models is that there isn't any recurring revenue. Recurring revenue is something that I think about a fair bit but I can't say that I have the best solution yet. In our case, we have all these users but we only see payment once. A subscription model would be great, but that's something really tough to pull off.

Q: I agree. A subscription model doesn't seem to be translating very well into the mobile world.

Why do you think this is the case though, considering that the model is so prevalent on the internet?

A: Honestly, I don't know. It's just not the norm, so it's difficult to make the case to a customer that your app is important enough to break the norm and charge them differently from every other app they've purchased before. I would love to hear your readers' thoughts on that question though.

Chapter: 10

Q: Haha. Let's see whether anyone steps up to answer that! Anyhow, we're just about done. Thanks for an informative interview!

A: No problem. Thanks for the interview as well. I really appreciate it!

9 Outsourcing Hacks For App Development

1) Obtain As Many Quotes As You Can

First off, you're going to want to obtain as many quotes as you can. If you don't have much experience in outsourcing, it's prudent to establish a 'logical' range of prices for the job at hand. For example, if you're hiring out the programming aspect and you've gotten quotes from a plethora of small development shops that vary from $20 to $5,000, with most of the quotes settling around the $2,000–$3,000 range, it's not rocket science to figure out that you're going to want to ditch both the $20 and $5,000 quote.

Undercutting and over-pricing too drastically could be signs of inexperience, and you don't want to risk the success of your app on a newbie. It could work out amazingly well or it could blow up in your face. Either way, if you're trying to minimize risk, it makes more sense to go with a contractor that has the business acumen not to price himself too far off the standard.

In addition, if you're using a third party site such as Odesk, Elance or Guru, you'll probably want to take note of the contractor's ratings and the number of jobs they've completed. Naturally, the higher the ratings and number of jobs completed, the better.

2) Interview Widely

You should be prepared to spend as long as it takes to find the right help. It makes sense to interview as many people as you can, especially if it's your first time outsourcing a job. Take a look at the portfolios of your potential hires and pick out those whose work gels with you. I personally make it a point to interview at least ten different candidates thoroughly on Skype for important jobs.

Austin L. Church uses a detailed list of questions to suss out potential candidates for every job. Always hire based on the person's ability to do the job as opposed to their personality. You're not trying to find a beer buddy here.

After you've narrowed down the field to two or three candidates, try to get in contact with a few of their previous clients. Find out what it's like working with these contractors. If you see that a contractor has developed a prominent mobile app, make sure you verify it. Some freelancers have been known to include fake client jobs in their portfolios. You'll also be surprised to find how disgruntled some of their previous clients can be, even if that same client gave them a 5-star review on Elance!

3) Make your Requirements Ridiculously Clear

You'll want your specifications to be ridiculously clear from the start. Your contractors base their quotes on your specifications, and loose, vague descriptions can lead to inaccurate quotes, or worse still, attempts to renege on work.

Your descriptions of what you want should be meticulous. You should also have wireframes of every single screen of your app. Anyone can learn to use simple wireframing tools. You don't have to be the slightest bit technical to be able to do so. You can use Powerpoint or Keynote to create simple mockups. You don't even have to pay for anything – if you don't have either, use a good ol' fashioned pen and paper!

Don't worry too much about anyone stealing your idea. The odds of that happening are slim to none. You can go the entire NDA

AppSource

route but honestly, it doesn't make that much of a difference. It's the execution of an idea that separates the men from the boys.

4) Hire The Best You Can Afford

This is particularly pertinent for your programmers and graphic designers. Bear in mind that if you're outsourcing most of the development of your app, you'll be entrusting what are arguably the most important assets of your business to the people you hire. You'll also be dealing with your freelancers frequently for what could be an extended period of time, depending on the complexity of your app.

It's not fun to end up in a situation where you have to hire someone else to patch up the shoddy work of a freelancer who didn't have the time, the inclination or the know-how to do a good job for you.

Telepathic Gaming originally tried to cut costs by hiring cheaper through popular outsourcing website, Elance. Unfortunately, they ended up being so unhappy with the quality of what they got, that they decided on a do-over for the code and graphical assets for their iOS game, *What It Takes*. This ended up costing them more time and money. If you're worried about whether a developer will be able to handle a big project, Andreas Kambanis suggests giving them a small programming task first and seeing how they perform.

While cost will always be a factor in any business decision, you'll have to balance the benefit of saving money against the possible risks and uncertainties of working with people from different cultures where speaking English doesn't come naturally. Remember–*Caveat Emptor* – let the buyer beware. The cheapest bidder isn't always the best bidder for you.

5) Always Negotiate

So you've narrowed the field down to a few contractors you like but that doesn't mean you have to settle on the prices they give you. Negotiate, negotiate, negotiate. You want to hire the best you can afford, *at the lowest price.*

Offer them a raving review for a job well done if your contractor is short on testimonials. If they're not willing to budge on price and you really like them, offer part of the payment in the form of a bonus *only* if you're satisfied with the job done.

Make a detailed plan about what you're willing to offer, and try to retain alternatives in case you need to walk away.

6) Use Project Management Tools to Manage your Project

Depending on the complexity of your app project, it may not be necessary for you to use sophisticated project management tools. Andrew Kambanis gets along fine communicating with his developers through Odesk and Elance.

However, if you're trying to build an app empire, and plan on hiring two or more freelance / full-time developers, using project management tools might make a bit more sense. Austin L. Church uses Basecamp, which has proven to be a pretty popular product over the years.

Once you get to the stage where you're trying to scale up an app business, both Mike Milo and Chad Mureta also believe that it's important to hire a project manager–someone who can handle the itty bitty details of the app development while you concentrate on the business side of things.

AppSource

7) Set Milestones

It's best to discuss thoroughly how payments will be made before you hire. Setting out a clear payment schedule with timed milestones is essential to keep track of progress and make sure you're not falling behind the curve.

Setting milestones ensures that you protect your cash and tells your contractor specifically what is expected from them according to the deadlines set out. Remember, you're not just picking dates out of thin air and assigning random goals. Make sure your milestones are easily measurable and realistic, and come to an agreement with your contractors that this is indeed the case.

8) Be 'Slow to Hire, Quick to Fire.'

Sometimes, even if you've done everything humanly possible to ensure you've gotten the right contractor, you still end up with a lemon. And while the life maxim advises you to 'make lemonade', that's something you absolutely do not want to be doing after hiring a dud.

In investing, the term usually used is 'cutting your losses'. Don't throw good money after bad. Once your contractor shows any sign of being a 'lemon', cut him/her loose and don't look back.

Some examples of 'lemon' behavior include:

- Taking excessively long to respond after being very prompt at the start. This is particularly prevalent with contractors who work in a different time-zone and ties in with...

- Putting your work on the backburner. Most contractors don't deal with only one client and you don't want to be the client that gets shafted. If they've missed your milestones by...well...a mile, at the very least, you'll want to have a serious talk with the help.

- Claiming to have implemented changes you requested despite not having done anything at all.

The app development world is rife with outsourcing horror stories, from the hired programmer who reuses bad code and refuses to change it, to the third world development shop that mysteriously disappears after working on your app for a month and a half.

As Austin L. Church says, he's running a business and he needs his contractors to deliver on time and within budget. If they aren't performing up to scratch, don't wait until it's too late to let them go.

9) There's More than One Way to Skin a Cat

Telepathic Gaming didn't have room in their budget for audio production and they didn't have the necessary expertise to do it themselves either. Caught between a rock and a hard place, they managed to outsource their audio production by enlisting the help of university students!

When push came to shove, Telepathic Gaming just couldn't afford to spend any more and had to think creatively in order to get the work done. It's possible to outsource work in myriad ways without looking at the usual suspects such as Elance, Odesk...and dare I say it, Fiverr.

AppSource

Get referrals from friends, approach universities, talk to people in communities/forums where designers, programmers or any other type of freelancer you're looking for hang out. In short, start hustling to get the best deals.

From Zero to Hero: How a Studio with no Experience in Mobile App Development Outsourced an iOS Game from Start to Finish

** Contributed by Telepathic Gaming, a mobile game development company founded by Ryan Mulrooney and Daniel Skinner **

It took us twelve months to finish development of our first iOS game, *What It Takes*, a round-based social word and number game for the iPhone and iPod Touch.

Our project was a relatively simple one. We had roughly around £7,500 budgeted for development and design to be outsourced, and we wanted the game to fulfill the following criteria:

- Have 3 different round types.

- Have players be able to earn XP points for performing well in the game. XP points would then amount to badges, titles and levels.

- Have players be able to complete challenges during gameplay.

- Contain a personal profile where player statistics and challenge awards are recorded.

This was the first time we had ever outsourced the development of an app, and the project didn't go as smoothly as we naively hoped it would. Shane kindly invited us to share our outsourcing experience so that anyone interested in hiring out their app development could gain some insights into mobile app development. In particular, outsourcing app development to countries (usually third-world) where work is relatively cheaper.

AppSource

We made a number of mistakes along the way, and hopefully our experience will help budding iOS game developers to avoid making said mistakes. We certainly don't consider ourselves experts, and all our advice stems from outsourcing the entirety of one iPhone game.

In the beginning we were a little ignorant of what we were doing, as most people with no prior experience usually are. Basically, we believed that after writing the requirements, the only work we would have to do was testing and marketing!

Unfortunately, from our experience, this wasn't and will probably never be the case. The outsourcing process is not a bed of roses but hopefully the following guidelines will help you to avoid some of the common pitfalls encountered.

The Nuts And Bolts Of Outsourcing an iPhone App.

Writing Your Requirements

You've got an idea for an iPhone app? Great! Now all you need to do is write the requirements for it. We found that using a wiki to write requirements was the easiest way to do it. A wiki has a nice layout and allows more than one person to work on the requirements simultaneously (from different locations). It is also extremely easy to structure the requirements and split up the different aspects of the app.

You can get started on creating a wiki here: http://www.mediawiki.org/wiki/MediaWiki

For an initial proof of concept, we created mock-up wireframes using a program called Balsamiq, and added these to our requirements in the wiki. The program allows you to create your own 'screenshots' by providing you with small graphical assets that you can add to create a rough pictorial image of what you want the actual game to look like. Because of the minimal 'sketch' style of these assets, they work really well as guidelines to create mental pictures of how you want your game to look.

Balsamiq worked really well for us, but it might not be for everyone. Fortunately, you can trial the program for one week before you commit to buying it. Aside from Balsamiq, there are also tons of other programs to help you wireframe your app – you can even use Powerpoint as a simple alternative, or if you want to be really old-school about it, you can draw out your wireframes on paper!

When writing your requirements, make sure they are as detailed as possible. Any screen that you imagine to be in the app, include it. This is essential for a few reasons:

- When attempting to outsource your work, companies will read your requirements and base their quote on that (well, in theory they should–but we didn't find that for the people we outsourced to. Good, respectable companies will though.)

- Because these companies will base their quote on your requirements, it serves as the perfect document to prove that certain work must be done–many a time the developers we outsourced to would complain that we were adding additional requirements. Having a 100-page document allowed us to quickly quash any complaints they had.

- It's important for you to understand your app inside out – only when you fully understand the intricacies of your app will you be able to get a true feel of whether it'll work or not.

Obtaining Quotes

At the start of the project, the only place we knew where cheaper developers and designers could be hired was Elance, a website that allows customers to connect with freelancers from around the world.

Whilst obtaining quotes, our main concern was the possibility of getting our game idea stolen. Initially, we were a little cagey about the information we allowed people to see. Our worries were basically futile–there are a few things you can do to reduce the chances of somebody stealing your idea, but the reality is that if anyone really wants to steal it, they can.

However, it doesn't really matter because at this stage, an idea is nothing more than just that – an idea. Proper implementation and execution of the development and marketing is what makes a mobile game a success.

Either way, the chances of having your idea stolen are extremely slim. The odds are against anyone out there eagerly waiting to make a game solely off the back of a game description from an unknown indie developer. There's just too much of a risk, and your simple game description doesn't convey enough details about your game. Someone might steal your idea once you have a working prototype, but stealing the idea before its birth is highly unlikely.

However, if you're still worried, there are safeguards you can employ:

- When creating your pitch on Elance (or any other outsourcing portal), don't give away any of the major details. E.g. For our pitch we noted that it was a 25 screen, social word and number game, with recorded statistics and XP points. At no point did we ever describe the mechanics of the rounds–it was just a simple, generic pitch.

- This might seem obvious but it's something that many developers seem to miss out. After receiving a quote from a company/freelancer, check out their portfolio. For any work you like the look of, try and contact the owner of the app, and ask them for some feedback on the developer/designer. That way you can verify their legitimacy. It also gives you a decent idea of the company's abilities, allowing you to make an informed decision before selection.

- After choosing the company, insist that they sign a Non-Disclosure Agreement (NDA). An NDA is basically a statement of intent. By signing it, the company agrees not to use or share any of the requirements they read.

The reality is that an NDA is practically worthless at this stage because you have nothing more than an idea. Fortunately, as mentioned earlier, it doesn't make business sense for most app development companies to rip off your ideas.

Choosing a Designer

So you've written your requirements document, and finally gotten over your fear of having your amazing game idea stolen. The next step, if you're outsourcing every aspect of your app, is to get yourself a graphic designer.

We made a few mistakes in hiring one, succeeding only in getting the work done for a low price. As the popular saying goes, 'When you pay peanuts, you get monkeys.' While we didn't pay much, the entire process was inefficient and we didn't obtain the top-quality graphics we wanted.

We used Elance, and chose a design company from Mumbai, India. They were reasonably priced, and had a decent portfolio, so we chose them. Big mistake. After four weeks it was evident that they would never complete the graphics–they had only completed the company logo and around 40% of the game's splash screen (there were 25 screens to design!), so we complained to Elance and our money was refunded.

You might wonder why we waited four weeks to officially complain. Well, it was simple naivete . They were adept at making excuses, and this being the first time we'd outsourced any sort of work, we weren't certain where we stood. We did complain frequently to the design company during these four weeks, but were always left wondering whether this was just the way outsourced freelance work went. It took us a while but we finally reported them to Elance, and terminated the contract.

Eager not to waste any more time (perhaps too eager), we immediately chose another company from Elance, this time a company from Canada that was a little more expensive. We chose this company because the main designer had been attentive with his messaging over Elance, and it was evident that he would be able to do the work quickly. The company didn't have much experience with iPhone app design but their normal illustrations were awesome, so we convinced ourselves that they should be able to do the job.

This wasn't really the case. They did get the job done quickly, but our previous fears of them not being able to produce suitable iPhone app graphics were quickly realized. After going back and forth a few times with our suggested improvements, it was evident that we would have to make the improvements ourselves.

Despite the poor work quality, they did finish all the work required, so we paid them and started trying to improve the graphics ourselves. We didn't have any experience with graphic design so progress was slow initially. Fortunately, after a month or so we were able to make the graphics look decent. Eventually, we settled most of the graphics ourselves.

TIPS:

1. If you've agreed on a timeline with the designer and it's obviously not going to be met, speak to them to see if there's an issue. If you sense bullshit, terminate the contract, get your money back and look elsewhere.

2. Familiarize yourself with whatever design tool your designers will be using. There's a high chance that the design you receive

won't be 100% to your liking (especially if the designer is quite cheap), so being familiar with the tool would make it easier to touch things up yourself.

3. At least have some idea how you would like your game to look. A cheap designer would likely be able to do the work as instructed, but won't be particularly creative. We initially found it difficult to envisage how the game should look, and only gave them a few pointers (e.g. We wanted a clock in the game logo, and wanted it to be blue), but after a couple of iterations, we gained a better understanding of what we wanted and could be more specific. If we'd had a clearer idea in the first place, we could have saved a little more time, and maybe gotten some assets that we actually wanted to keep. I'm still not convinced a massive amount of quality would have been delivered in our case though.

Choosing a Developer

Despite the bad experience we had with the Indian designers, budget constraints led to us choosing yet another Indian company from Kolkata. An old work colleague of ours actually lives in Kolkata, and acted as a middleman in finding this company for us, and negotiating a lower price. In retrospect, we could have probably used a company from Elance for a similar amount.

Again, it didn't start particularly well–they spent almost a month perusing our requirements, only to send us back a project plan that was basically the titles of each of the sections of our requirements!

Initially, we decided to pay through Elance for some payment security, but after a couple of months, we decided to avoid the Elance commission by paying our old work colleague directly. He was taking his own cut from each payment we made, so we were convinced it was in his interest not to take the money himself. At that point, the payment plan between us became a gentleman's agreement, where we would pay at the end of each completed milestone.

This was definitely not the best way to do things as it left both parties vulnerable. At any point the company could just walk and discontinue working, taking the code with them, and conversely, we could walk at any moment without paying for completed work. However, it did help us to complete the project on our low budget.

Issues Faced

The problems we had with these Indian developers were so numerous we'd never be able to list them all. But here's a rundown of some of the more notable issues we encountered:

- They always say 'yes'. Never take 'yes' for an answer as quite often, 'yes' means 'no'. They agreed with everything, even when they didn't understand. Eventually we made it a point to make them repeat back the requirements we'd discussed, and gave them tests to see whether they'd actually understood.

- They rarely ask questions. Don't ever assume that just because they are working, they are working on the correct thing. We wasted at least eight weeks of project time by allowing them to work without constantly holding their hand. Unfortunately for us, they didn't understand the requirements and developed something completely different from what we wanted! We never made that mistake again.

- A tip here would be to insist on a daily build if you can. The longer they develop the app without your supervision, the higher the chance of something being incorrect. Getting a

AppSource

daily build allows you to find issues early before they become a big problem.

- Always be explicit with your requirements. The few times we didn't write exactly how we wanted something to be developed and just assumed that they'd do it properly–they never did. For example, when a player finishes a game, that game tile goes into a 'Game Over' section, so that players can see their previous results (win, lose, draw). A player can also resign from a game, obviously (to us) resulting in a loss for them. The development house didn't see it that way; they didn't know what to do with it and didn't think to ask, so they just made the tile disappear completely from both players' screens! Now that would have been a great user experience.

- They copy and paste most of their code, meaning that if you ask to make a change in one place, don't expect that change to be made in another. Our game has 2 different game modes– Single Player and Online. Both contain instruction pages. These instructions were misaligned and so we raised a generic 'instructions misaligned' bug expecting it to be fixed on both. Nope! Only in Online Mode. There were countless incidents like this.

- Expect things to go wrong on completely unrelated code. After every build we would regression test the whole thing–despite them only having worked on something totally unrelated. (E.g. A few times they'd be working on something in the game rounds, which would then somehow cause the game to crash when trying to create a new account!)

In the end, after months of delay and very poor quality work, we were forced to cancel the arrangement with the developers and rewrite the code entirely from scratch. You might think this was crazy after we had spent so much money and time with these developers. However, we weren't willing to have our idea spoiled by terrible implementation.

We knew that the code was so poor we would have no hope of trying to maintain it if and when something went wrong. As with the graphics, if you want a job done properly, you really need to do it yourself, or be incredibly careful when taking the cheap option.

Depending on your budget, it might be a good idea to pay a little more and go local. You'll speak the same language in the same time zone. Don't underestimate how important this can be.

Managing the Project

As with any development project, you are inevitably going to find some defects in the code (in our case there were 764). Keeping track and prioritizing all those defects becomes almost impossible without proper bug tracking software.

I mean, how would you effectively manage them? A spreadsheet? Email? Keeping track of 764 defects in such a manner would have been impossible! There are plenty of bug tracking tools out there, all with varying degrees of complexity. Thankfully, a decent number of them are free (or very cheap), so this is one less project cost that you'll have to incur. Choosing the right bug tracking software is based purely on the project you want to lead. We looked at two–JIRA and Mantis, and decided on Mantis.

Without getting into too much detail, JIRA is excellent (it costs $10 for 10 users, which should probably be enough for most indie projects) – it allows you and your developers to accurately plan out each milestone by splitting the project into smaller developments, including estimates, which gives you a perfect picture of where

AppSource

your project is going.

When a piece of work is completed, the testers are automatically notified, and testing can commence. In short, it's a great tool for project management and agile development, but it would have been pointless for our project. We wanted to use it, but getting the developers to learn how to use it properly would have been a waste of time.

So, we decided on Mantis, a simpler bug-tracking tool, which we could just use to raise bugs and set priorities – something easy for our developers to learn to use. Mantis does have some minor reporting features but it's basically just a bug tracker. It's incredibly simple to use, and the developers from Kolkata didn't have any problems using it either.

Here are the links:

JIRA – http://www.atlassian.com/software/ji.../?tab=download

Mantis–http://www.mantisbt.org/download.php

Audio Production

Unfortunately, the cost of audio production (game sounds, music, etc) wasn't something we had budgeted for, and as a result we weren't able to afford it. To remedy this, we decided to try and enlist the help of some university students from a Sound Production course, on an internship.

This worked really well for us, and in hindsight we should have tried to get more aspects of the game designed in this way. We made a simple but professional post including the game logo and game description, and explained exactly what sounds we wanted. We then emailed this to each of the local universities in our area. The response was incredible! We had over 200 replies from students, and also a few replies from tutors who were interested!

Eventually we chose a guy whose sample sounds were really impressive. Fortunately he was from our nearest city, so we met up with him, and discussed exactly where we thought the game was going and the type of sounds that would be appropriate. He went away and did what was asked, and after a few suggestions of amendments from us, we had a full suite of game sounds in 2 weeks. That was definitely the most painless part of the whole process, and we'll definitely be using him again for future projects.

Here's a general tip–when trying to enlist an intern, be careful what time of year you do it. It's a fact that students are lazy most of the time, but they do occasionally have more work to do during certain parts of the year. We sent out our email requesting for interns in the middle of the school term, so the students had already passed that hectic first month of a new year, and had some spare time.

We tried using this same approach for video production, but found almost zero success! We sent the email right at the start of term (unfortunately for us, this was when we needed the video to be done), and got very few responses. I had no responses from any of the tutors to indicate that they had forwarded on the email to their students. After a follow up email, I received a response from 2 students–neither of which was suitable. Evidently, timing is crucial.

Video Production

Again, we made a few mistakes. First of all we tried to enlist the help of an intern, as mentioned above, and failed. After this minor setback we looked elsewhere for a company to create the video,

AppSource

and eventually found a Belgian company to do it.

Their videos looked really stylish to us, and they certainly seemed to have the production skills that we were looking for. Once again, we thought that because we were paying a company to create a stylish video, they would be able to do so, and create the perfect video, with very little guidance.

So we sent them a shell script and waited for our perfect video to arrive. Needless to say, we didn't get the desired results. We then thought long and hard about the style and production we wanted and fed this back to the company. After a few iterations, we got a style that we liked and we were fairly happy with the footage, so we paid them.

It was only after collecting other people's feedback that we realized there were certain errors in the footage that would cost us more money if we wanted to have it corrected and re-recorded. Thus, as with programming and design, it helps to be as detailed as possible with your specifications from the start.

App Icon Design

We tried to get our original designer to create an app icon for us, but it wasn't to the standard that we desired, so we decided to hire another freelance designer instead. Feeling a little dissatisfied with the quality of workers on Elance (just from personal experience–I'm sure there are many success stories!), we didn't fancy going through them again. It also didn't help that we didn't have any idea how we wanted our app icon to look like. This meant we couldn't put all our faith in one designer–because they might not deliver the goods.

As we were uncertain of what we wanted, we decided the best way forward was to see as many different designs as possible. Enter

99 Designs. On 99designs.com, you post what job you would like completed, set what price you are willing to pay, and then any designers who see the job and are interested will design for you for free—you then pay for the winning design.

This method worked perfectly for us. Around 30 designers submitted ideas. We looked at those ideas and suggested changes to the designers whose ideas we liked and eventually chose a Bulgarian designer. The quality of her work was amazing! She was also a breeze to collaborate with, and produced great designs at reasonable prices.

Conclusion

Hopefully, our experience has provided a little insight to some of the mess-ups that can occur when you're outsourcing the development of almost every single element of a mobile app/game. We've learnt a great deal along the way and definitely won't be making the same mistakes again with our next app!

About the Author

Shane Lee lives in Singapore, where his innate talent for drinking copious amounts of coffee goes largely unnoticed.

He runs the website Beginning iOS Dev, and is the co-founder of Innately Curious Media.

An author, writer, entrepreneur and all around good guy, he tends to look pretty grumpy in author bios.

For accompanying interviews, and additional information on iPhone app development, pop on by to www.beginningiosdev.com

Questions Or Comments?

I appreciate feedback, and I'd love to hear your thoughts.

Email me at admin@beginningiosdev.com

Enjoyed Reading This Book? Check Out More Books By The Author:

The App Store Playbook: Discover How 10 Successful iPhone App Developers Hit It Big Selling Games On The App Store

Cost-Effective App Marketing: The Tight-Wad Mobile Developer's Quick and Easy Guide To Promoting iOS Apps

Printed in Great Britain
by Amazon.co.uk, Ltd.,
Marston Gate.